PLANNING GUIDELINES FOR
MIDDLE SCHOOL EDUCATION

PLANNING GUIDELINES FOR MIDDLE SCHOOL EDUCATION

JON WILES

University of Texas
at Arlington

KH

KENDALL/HUNT PUBLISHING COMPANY
Dubuque, Iowa

Copyright © 1976 by Kendall/Hunt Publishing Company

Library of Congress Catalog Card Number: 76—19245

ISBN 0—8403—1531—7

Printed in the United States of America

The biological changes occuring in the individual during the preadolescent period are easily recognized by even a casual observer of students at this age. Students are distinguished by gross differences in size, coordination, sexual maturation, and energy levels. A 1972 White House Panel on Youth made the following observation: "From eleven through sixteen or seventeen years the range of individual differences in physical structure and physiological function at any given chronological age is greater than at any other time in the human life span."

Internally, the body is undergoing both glandular and hormonal readjustments, long bone growth, and the activation of sexual reproductive organs. External manifestations of these internal changes are rapid growth spurts, development of secondary sexual characteristics, periods of extreme awkwardness, and a wide range of emotional moods.

Our observations of both behavior and reasoning capacity during these years suggest that preadolescence is a major period of growth in intellectual development. The most widely cited model of intellectual development in children, to date, is one first stated by Jean Piaget nearly sixty years ago. Piaget hypothesized stages of growth and capacity in the development of the mental processes, and during the period of preadolescence Piaget proposed a change in capacity which would allow for greater abstract reasoning. According to Piaget, there is a movement away from a total dependence of what is perceived and experienced in the immediate environment during preadolescence, and an emerging capacity to deal with intellectual abstractions. The Piaget model has generally been supported by other recognized research on intellectual development.

In addition to new capacities and dimensions of intellectual development, other signs of growth can be anticipated during this preadolescent stage. There is, for example, an expansion in the range of interests during this time. Imagination is often well developed by this period. There is a heightened curiosity about adult roles and relationships. There is a concern with meaning and values. In some children there is an emergence of unusual talents.

Changes in social roles and sociability in general are dramatic during the preadolescent period. The stage of development is one of great introspection and interest in "self." The self-concept, often described as the "invisible price tag" one holds for himself, is being redefined and is affected by both outward body image and peer acceptance. Feelings of adequacy and worthiness are characteristically irregular.

Because of social instability, peer groups and cliques are established and promoted to provide support and stability. Conformity and allegiance to group values become paramount concerns for preadolescents, and often are sources of friction at home and in school. The student at this age finds himself in a paradoxical situation: while he is striving to establish in-

2

1

THE EMERGENCE OF THE MIDDLE SCHOOL

During this century intermediate school literature has repeatedly made substantial arguments for a program of education structured around the developmental needs of preadolescents. These arguments, first based on common sense observations, have grown stronger as the social sciences have become more sophisticated in understanding the ramifications of human growth and development. While educators have acknowledged the preadolescent period in their writings for seventy years, only recently have we come to appreciate the critical nature of this period in the development of healthy and functioning adults. For society, with its concerns for productive social behavior, this formative period is crucial.

The period of human development between late childhood and the adolescent stage has been referred to as preadolescence, transescence, and the early teen period. It can be described and analyzed from a number of vantage points. Physically, it is a time ranging from the onstart of pubescent development until physical maturity is acknowledged. From the perspective of social growth, this period spans a time from a state of complete dependence in childhood to a quasi-independent status in full adolescence. Psychologically, this stage of development represents a time of adjustment and basic realignment in terms of reference groups and allegiances.

The overall nature of the preadolescent stage of development is one of immense and comprehensive change for the individual. In some societies, such dramatic change is symbolized by a cultural ritual. In the American society, the preadolescent period is dominated by both stress and tension due to the blurring of cultural roles and expectations.

If the preadolescent stage is characterized by marked physical changes in the body, changes which in turn spark other less observable alterations in the individual, then the chronological age during which most American children experience preadolescence is ten to fourteen. Growth studies conducted at the University of California at Berkeley found that nearly ninety-five percent of all children experience the onset of puberty during these ages. The exact age at which an individual enters or exits preadolescence appears to be determined by both physical and environmental factors.

1

INTRODUCTION

For three-quarters of a century American educators have spoken of a program of education particularly suited to the needs of students between late childhood and adolescence. Both the junior high school, and more recently the middle school, have sought to provide such a special program. While theoretical descriptions of such a program have been abundant, few of the student-centered ideas have found their way into intermediate classrooms. This unfortunate state of affairs appears to be the result of two conditions. First, there is a significant lack of understanding about the role of education at this level. Second, educators in the intermediate schools have repeatedly failed to use planning to move from theory to practice.

In terms of comprehension of educational purpose, few intermediate educators have been able to resist the lure of content-based curriculums in responding to the needs of preadolescents. Though paying lip-service to the developmental needs of students at this level, educators have been unwilling to utilize such needs as planning bases for the curriculum. After all this time, we still fail to make the basic connection between the needs of students and the role of education. This understanding is essential to implementing quality programs in the middle grades.

In terms of development, the inability of most intermediate schools to go beyond rhetoric in addressing the needs of students in the middle grades may indicate the absence of primary planning skills. To attempt to implement a complex student-directed program of education without long-range planning is folly. The number of critical variables to be considered in such an action makes it imperative that development be well planned. Educational activity in the middle grades reflects a continued failure to employ such planning tools.

With these two conditions in mind, *Planning Guidelines for Middle School Education* has been compiled. The materials herein represent an attempt to state succinctly the meaning of the middle school movement, and to provide some basic planning guidelines for putting theory into practice. It is hoped that these few ideas will enable dedicated middle school educators to become more effective in developing educational programs for those students between late childhood and adolescence.

CONTENTS

Introduction vii

Chapter 1   The Emergence of the Middle School 1

2   A Program Design for Middle School Education 13

3   Planning Considerations in the Development of Middle
Schools 25

4   Instruction in the Middle School. 49

5   The Evaluation of Middle School Programs 71

Appendix: Faces in the Crowd 81

dependence, he also needs the security of being able to revert back to childhood behaviors.

At school, one difficult phase of social developnent for most preadolescents is the establishment of stable relationships with the opposite sex. Trading in like-sex associations for opposite-sex associations is aggrevated considerably by the uneven physical development of girls and boys at this stage, as well as by the social expectations of parents.

At home the preadolescent experiences an ever-growing need to break away from dependency on parents and family and to establish new status roles. Because of the redefinition of such roles, and the corresponding expected behaviors, social development is notably uneven. Development in social growth is characterized by erratic behavior and contradictory reasoning patterns.

The emotional dimension of development is a composite of physical, intellectual and social growth. While complex, this area of development is vitally important in terms of social needs and expectations for the educational process.

Like intellectual development, most of what is known about emotional growth during this stage of development has been gained by observation. This period is known to be, especially in our society, one of great stress and contrasts. Inconsistent behavior, a reflection of inner emotional pulls, is prevalent. Moods ranging from ecstasy to severe depression, from anger and aggression to affection and complacency are common to the classroom. Events at home, in school, or enroute, can trigger unpredictable responses.

A factor of extreme importance to educational planners is a recognition of the fact that many social agencies dealing with problems of adult deviancy identify the preadolescent period as a crucial formative period. The criminal, the alcoholic, the insane, the uninvolved nonproductive adult . . . all are felt to first overtly display these tendencies as they enter preadolescence.

Without question, the totality of physical, intellectual, social, and emotional changes occuring during this period of growth and development make the preadolescent a unique individual. It is probable that there is no other time in life when an individual must experience so many changes so quickly without the benefit of either experience or precedence. Education, formal and cultural, can affect the direction and outcome of such changes.

A school program can either facilitate a smooth passage through this period of development by making the appropriate curricular arrangements, or it can aggrevate an already stressful condition by being and acting insensitive to the preadolescent learner. There can be little doubt that the events of preadolescence affect school performance and, in turn, are affected by school programs.

Viewing the role and purpose of school from this comprehensive perspective suggests that the structure and methods of educating the preadolescent must be carefully considered. If our overall view is centered on the desire to assist each individual in finding his place in the organized society, then we must realize that the experiences a preadolescent has in the middle grades will greatly contribute to his ability to adjust and contribute.

The Middle School Movement

For the past sixty-five years intermediate education in America has been dominated by the junior high school, an institution established and developed to serve students in the preadolescent years. During its history the junior high school made numerous significant contributions to education in the middle years. Through its establishment, a special level of educating was created. Through its organization the American public came to recognize and accept a major group of young persons in our society. Through its programs, the definition of education was broadened.

Yet, in the long run, the junior high school failed in its purpose; it never really served the developmental needs of those students for which it was created. In spite of its programs, it was often irrelevant to the lives of those preadolescents in attendance. By the early 1960s a growing frustration with the institution prompted the search for an alternative form of schooling. As descriptions of this alternative grew increasingly numerous, the label "middle school" seemed to stick. By the late sixties, the name "middle school" was being used in numerous books, articles, and surveys as something distinct from the junior high school.

A point of confusion for anyone reading the respective literature of the junior high school and the middle school, literature separated by a full fifty years, is their striking similarity. Not only is the rhetoric nearly identical, but the sequence of their concern is regularly parallel. To extract statements from these two periods of educational development is to experience a form of pedagogical reincarnation. It is perfectly understandable, therefore, that the middle school emergence is often misunderstood.

Perhaps the single most important difference between the junior high school and the middle school programs is the focus of their organization and operation. Whereas both institutions draw their rationale from the developmental needs of preadolescent learners, the junior high school has maintained a traditional content-based design while the middle school has organized itself according to the developmental needs of learners. In a sense, the middle school represents an educational design which has been constructed to allow an educational philosophy to be implemented.

It is unfortunate that comparisons between the junior high school and the middle school have been drawn in terms of either/or thinking, because in reality neither institution is pure in terms of content-focus or student-

4

focus. Nonetheless, if a continuum existed between these two foci in terms of day-to-day decision making, the middle school would consistently appear on the student side of the philosophical watershed and the junior high school would most often align itself and its priorities on the content side of the continuum.

This philosophical understanding is crucial for anyone interested in the middle school concept, because the middle school is not simply a basket for the latest innovation or a connection between the discontinued programs of the elementary and high schools. The rationale of the middle school cannot survive if it is residual in nature. It was at this point that the junior high school failed. Because the junior high school was first and foremost a "junior" high school, with an organization and program structured around "junior" high school content and activity, it was unable to effectively focus upon the developmental needs of its students. It became irrelevant and often dysfunctional to the lives of its students.

The middle school, then, represents a renewed effort to design and implement a program of education which can accomodate the needs of the preadolescent population. It is a broadly-focused program of education drawing its philosophy and rationale from the evolving body of knowledge concerned with human growth and development. The middle school represents a systematic effort to organize the schooling experience in a way which will facilitate the maximum growth and development of all learners.

The middle school program consists of arrangements and activities which attempt to tie formal learning directly to the developmental needs of the students being served. To date, identified "developmental tasks" represent the most promising criteria for curriculum development which will intersect school activity with learner growth and development.

Developmental Tasks

The school does not represent our society's only mechanism for preservation and adaptation. The family, the church, and the media, to name a few other mechanisms, all contribute to the educative processes of the society. The public school, however, still remains the only formal sanctioned institution in America which was created and is supported to preserve and promote the society.

A problem which has plagued educational planners throughout this century in America is how to determine the scope of the school's responsibility in educating children. As social, economic, and political forces have acted on our nation, the dimension of school operation and the role of the school has fluctuated. In this last quarter of the twentieth century, the scope of school responsibilities is immense. The educative process has expanded to involve fifteen to twenty times as many individuals each day as were in

5

the armed services of the nation during our most recent war. With such size has come increasing diversity of both responsibility and concern.

Obviously, public schools in America cannot continue to expand their concerns and commitments indefinitely. They must, through their program planning, identify those areas which can be dealt with within the boundaries of available resources. Schools must develop a focus, a criteria for the determination of the curriculum.

One thrust in attempting to pin down the areas in which the school might have primary responsibilities in working with young people of all backgrounds and capacities has been the identification of "developmental tasks" of growth. From observed by sociologist Robert Havighurst in the early 1950s, the various developmental tasks of human growth represent universal steps in a culture toward the achievement of adulthood. An assumption made in considering developmental tasks as a possible criteria for school planning, and one essential to the acceptance of the middle school rationale, is that the comprehensive development and expansion of human potential is both important and a concern of the school.

During the past twenty years developmental psychologists, educators, sociologists, and others have identified many "tasks" regularly encountered by all individuals in our society as they progress from childhood to adolescence. Examples of such tasks are on the following page.

While these developmental tasks are only suggestive of the kinds of concerns and needs experienced by young persons between early childhood and adolescence, they do indicate some areas where school programs can intervene meaningfully in the developmental process.

At the early childhood-elementary level, representing the corresponding school years from nursery school through the third grade, there might be a focus on the following kinds of need areas:

1. *Social Adjustment.* An introduction of institutional living, a building of relationships with other children and adults, the encouragement of socially acceptable behaviors.
2. *Initial Physical Development.* The encouragement of both gross motor skills and specialized tasks associated with the schooling process. Also, the detection and correction of progress-retarding deficiencies, such as visual and learning problems.
3. *An Awareness of Self.* The establishment and awareness of identity as an individual. The development of autonomy, an exploration of roles, the discovery of interests and talents.
4. *Academic Readiness.* Consisting of learning basal knowledge, development of learning skills, establishing symbols literacy, promoting positive attitudes toward schooling.

Examples of Developmental Tasks

Adolescence
Emancipation from parent-dependency
Occupational projection- selection
Completion of value structure
Acceptance of self

Preadolescence
Handling major body changes
Asserting independence from family
Establishing sex role identity
Dealing with peer group relationships-
Controlling emotions
Constructing a values foundation
Pursuing interest expression
Utilizing new reasoning capacities
Developing acceptable self-concept

Late Childhood
Mastering communication skill
Building meaningful peer relations
Thinking independently
Acceptance of self
Finding constructive expression outlets
Role projection

Middle Childhood
Structuring the physical world
Refining language and thought patterns
Establishing relationships with others
Understanding sex roles

Early Childhood
Developing motor control
Emerging self-awareness
Mapping out surroundings
Assigning meaning to events
Exploring relationships with others
Developing language and thought patterns

7

5. *Sensory Development.* Encouraging expansion of the five senses including aesthetic appreciation and an awareness of environmental beauty.*

    In the intermediate years, corresponding to the middle grades of school, 4-8, the focus of programs might be:

1. *Social Development and Refinement.* To facilitate the acceptance of new roles and responsibilities, to teach the interdependence of individuals in society, to explore social values, to teach basic communications and human relations skills.
2. *Promotion of Physical and Mental Health.* An intensive program of exercise designed to develop conditioning and coordination. An accompanying component used to promote positive physical and mental health practices. Basic sex education.
3. *Development of Self-Concept and Self-Acceptance.* To promote feelings of worth in all individuals, to accentuate strengths, to aid in the development of realistic perceptions and expectations of self, to foster increased independence, to assist in values exploration, to explore and expand interests.
4. *Academic Adequacy.* To insure literacy, to aid in the organization needed for academic achievement, to teach skills for continued learning, to introduce knowledge areas, to explore career potentials as they relate to interests, to develop independence and autonomy in learning, to foster critical thinking.
5. *Aesthetic Stimulation.* To develop latent talents in art, music, writing, to promote an understanding of man's aesthetic achievement, to develop a capacity for the satisfying use of leisure time.*

    In the secondary school, corresponding to the first years of the high school and perhaps into the first postsecondary years (9-13), the following program focus might be utilized:

1. *Social Maturation.* Promoting increased independence and autonomy in decision making, an exploration of the rights and responsibilities of adulthood and citizenship, a study of marriage and family life, an exploration of socially-acceptable means of communication.
2. *Refinement of Health.* Defining and analyzing the meaning of good health for individuals and society, the personalizing of positive health plans, an emphasis on programs of individual health development and maintenance, a study of causation of poor health (drugs, alcoholism, smoking, obesity).

*No priority for importance is intended by the order of these categories.

3. *Supporting Self-Actualization.* Assisting in value clarification, exploration of careers and education as extensions of individual needs and interests, the correction of severe psychological and emotional problem areas, the identification and emphasis of personal strengths.
4. *Academic Specialization.* The development of specialization in knowledge areas and learning skills, an exploration of academic opportunities, the refinement of critical and analytical thinking, an emphasis on the utility of knowledge of everyday living.
5. *Aesthetic Refinement.* The pursuit of quality living, an emphasis of social existence, the refinement of aesthetic talents, the development of satisfying hobbies, an understanding of man's capacities for further achievements.*

Utilization of the developmental tasks experienced by all young persons in our society as a criteria for planning school programs suggests some global areas of focus for activity development. Outlined below are some continuums of concern:

E.C.E.—Elementary	Intermediate	Secondary
Social adjustment	Social Development	Social Maturation
Initial Physical Development	Promotion of Physical Development	Refinement of Physical Health
Self-Awareness	Self-Acceptance	Self-Actualization
Academic Readiness	Academic Adequacy	Academic Specialization
Sensory Development	Aesthetic Stimulation	Aesthetic Refinement

〉-----------Continuums of Growth in School------------〉

While each level of education must make a thorough analysis of the needs of the students assigned to their care, it is interesting to view in isolation the tasks and possible roles of schooling at the intermediate level of education:

Tasks	School Roles
Late Childhood	1. *Social development and refinement*
Mastery of communication	Acceptance of responsibility
Building peer relationships	Interdependence of individuals
Thinking as an individual	Exploration of social values

*No priority of importance is intended by the order of these categories.

9

Tasks	School Roles
Acceptance of self	Human relations
Finding means of expression	Communications skills
Role projection	2. *Promotion of physical and mental health*
Preadolescence	Conditioning and coordination
Handling physical change	
Asserting independence	Understanding of hygiene
Establishing sex-role identity	Sex education
Refining peer relationships	Understanding nutrition
Controlling emotions	
Constructing a values foundation	3. *Develop self-concept and self-acceptance*
Pursuing interest	
Use of reasoning capacity	Accentuate strengths
Developing self-concept	Self-analysis
	Increased responsibility
	Values exploration
	Interest expansion
	4. *Academic adequacy*
	Basic literacy
	Org. for academic achievement
	Skills for continued learning
	Introduce knowledge areas
	Explore career potential
	Develop learning autonomy
	Critical thinking
	5. *Aesthetic stimulation*
	Develop latent talents
	Promote aesthetic appreciation
	Develop leisure time activities

The matching of some of the developmental tasks of late childhood and preadolescence with some of the possible roles of the school during the corresponding grade levels highlights interesting conditions now existing in intermediate education. Few programs in the middle grades, it appears, could justify their experiences in terms of the needs of students now being served. The narrowness of the curriculum in most intermediate schools is a historical hybrid derived from other levels of schooling.

If educational planners choose to use the developmental needs of the students being served as a criteria for curriculum development, the school must broaden its definition of an "education." There must be a greater concern of social and emotional dimensions of preadolescent development,

10

since academic preparation and physical development represent only part of the needs of emerging adolescents.

Our growing awareness of the affective dimensions of learning, such as feelings, attitudes, and emotions, suggest that we must deal with preadolescents in a more sophisticated and comprehensive manner. We can no longer afford to ignore the environmental conditions surrounding the schooling process. Further, we must acknowledge that our objectives in formal schooling require altered behaviors as well as a growth in intellect.

It seems obvious that the kinds of administrative and curricular arrangements made by the school at both the building and classroom level will need to be rethought and redesigned. Greater program flexibility and diversity will have to be introduced in all facets of school life. Activity will have to be broadened and enriched.

Chapter Summary

Since its inception, the intermediate level of education in America has been rationalized in terms of human growth and development, and more specifically in terms of service to a very special learner. As the result of the failure of the junior high school to respond programmatically to the needs of preadolescents, the middle school has evolved. The middle school represents a renewed effort to establish a program of education based on a human growth and development rationale. It is an attempt to implement a philosophy of educating.

According to the middle school philosophy, educators must study the developmental patterns of students in the preadolescent stage of development in order to structure a meaningful program of education. A means must be found to intersect the larger goals of educating with the needs of the individual. The developmental tasks engaged in by all students during the stage of growth provides planners with one possible universal criteria for program development which will benefit every student.

Once educational planners gain consensus on the global goals of educating, and agreement on the capabilities and limitations of available resources, they face the difficult job of designing educational experiences to achieve desired ends. For the most part, educators in the middle grades in the past have shown little imagination in designing school programs to meet avowed goals.

The development of a curriculum in the middle school must flow from the global objectives of intermediate education; to serve a special learner in a specific stage of development. Planners must squarely face the question, "what kinds of learning experiences will promote the individual growth and

11

development of the preadolescent learner?" Beyond understanding of the goals of the middle school lies a process of planning and development.

SUGGESTED READINGS

Arth, Alfred A. "Directing the Young Adolescent Toward Becoming a Significant Other." Working paper distributed at National Middle School Conference, Columbus, Ohio, 1974.

Bough, Max. "Theoretical and Practical Aspects of the Middle School." *NASSP Bulletin,* LIII, 335, March, 1969.

Coleman, James. "How the Young Become Adults." *Phi Delta Kappan,* LIV, 4, December, 1972.

Dettre, John R. "The Middle School: A Separate and Equal Entity." *The Clearinghouse,* XLVII, 1, September, 1973.

Eichhorn, Donald H. "Middle School in the Making." *Educational Leadership,* XXI, 3, December, 1973.

Flavell, J. *The Developmental Psychology of Jean Piaget.* Princeton, N.J.: Van Nostrand, 1963.

Georgiady, Nicholas P. "The Emergence of the Middle School." *Midwest Middle School Journal,* II, 3, June, 1973.

Hannan, Thomas P. "Middle School: The Need to Establish a Unique Identity." *Middle School Journal,* 1, Spring, 1974.

Havighurst, Robert J. "The Middle School Child in Contemporary Society" *Theory Into Practice,* VII, 3, June, 1968.

Havighurst, Robert J. *Developmental Tasks and Education* New York: Longmans, Green, 1952.

Kagan, Jerome. "A Conception of Early Adolescence." *National Elementary Principal,* LI, November, 1971.

Ogletree, Earl J. "Intellectual Growth in Children." *Phi Delta Kappan,* LV, 6, February, 1974.

Soares, Louise M. and Anthony T. "Self-Perceptions of Middle School Pupils." *Elementary School Journal,* 36, 6, April, 1973.

Thornburg, Hershal (ed.) *Preadolescent Development,* University of Arizona Press, 1974.

White House Conference on Youth. "Adolescence: Youth in Transition." Report of the Panel on Youth, 1972 Proceedings.

Wilson, Mildred T. "The Middle School Defined Now: Freedom to Behave." *Dissemination Services,* V, 9, June, 1974.

NOTES

2

A PROGRAM DESIGN FOR MIDDLE SCHOOL EDUCATION

Any curriculum design, really a plan for interaction with students, is based upon assumptions about how learning occurs. When such assumptions are formalized, they become a theory of learning. For planners in the middle school to develop an effective design for education, they must first clarify beliefs about how learning is thought to occur. Throughout this century, intermediate school literature has repeatedly linked school learning for the preadolescent with developmental activities of the period. From the literature, three recurring beliefs can be extracted concerning preadolescent learning:

1. Learning is natural and on-going in preadolescence.
2. Learning revolves around adjustment and self-acceptance in preadolescence.
3. Learning is a highly individual act in preadolescence.

The idea that learning is natural and on-going during preadolescence is based on the understanding that persons of this age group must relearn many of the things thought to be mastered in childhood. Not only is there a major readjustment of physical skills, but also ones concerning perceptions and beliefs. Learning is natural in preadolescence because it is required to complete the growth transition.

The idea that learning revolves around adjustment and self-acceptance in preadolescence refers to the "ordering" of change occuring at this time. As the preadolescent changes, so too does his perceived world. Getting "his world" back into order is a prime concern of students from ten to fourteen years old. It can also be a significant source of motivational energy, both inside and outside of school.

The idea that learning in preadolescence is highly individual refers to the process by which learning opportunities are selected. Because the development of early teens is uneven and occuring in many dimensions of growth, individual learners select or focus on those activities and opportunities thought to be important to themselves. In a sense, learners at this age "preset" or control the reception of learning by where they choose to focus their attention.

Because of this condition, learner interaction with a learning situation in school will be uniquely personal. Understanding of this teaching-learning condition in preadolescence can change our way of thinking about a school; from a place where teaching occurs to a place where personal learning is occuring. Our century-old attempt to depersonalize and standardize education in the intermediate school makes little sense when the full range of learner development and needs are considered.

These three beliefs about learning in preadolescence, drawn from the literature of the intermediate school, provide additional guidance in our attempt to design a program of education for the middle school. When coupled with the general rationale of intermediate education, the middle school becomes: a program constructed around the unique developmental needs of preadolescents, featuring a natural, individualized program focused on **Self.**

Goals of the Program

One of the great difficulties in designing a middle school program is to discover the essential or key elements as opposed to the myriad of arrangements found in such schools. The planner is often confronted with a perplexing series of cues as suggested by the list below:

Planning for Personal Development

Nongradedness   Team Teaching

Parent Involvement   Independent Study

Community Education   Flexible Scheduling

Promotion of Humaness   Open-Space Buildings

Varied Learning Materials   Self-Concept Development

Interest-Centered Activities   Interdepartmental Curriculums

Individualized Instruction   Multi-Diminsional Evaluation

Values Clarification   Differentiated Staffing

Intramural Programs   Humanizing Education

Teacher-Counselors   Multi-Age Grouping

Learning Centers   Peer Counseling

Exploratory-Interest Curriculums

A typical reaction of educators viewing the middle school curriculum from a comprehensive perspective is to be overwhelmed by the number of critical elements. At first, middle schools appear to form an umbrella over all sorts of curricular arrangements. To ferret out the essential structure of the curriculum, to differentiate between goals (ends) and arrangements (means), is a planning prerequisite for implementing a substantive middle school curriculum.

Returning to the dominant theme of middle school programs stated previously, to facilitate personal growth and adjustment during the pre-adolescent period, we can identify some key characteristics or elements of the curriculum regardless of local conditions and resources. These characteristics or elements, collectively, define a framework for the curricular design.

Key Elements of the Middle School Program

The following elements are essential to the middle school program and, as such, should direct decision making and evaluation of individual middle school curriculum:

1. A program concerned with the total development of the learner
2. A program focused upon the individual student
3. A program featuring individualized learning
4. A program planned around the needs and interests of the learner
5. A program humane in nature and emphasizing success and personal growth
6. A program emphasizing guidance and counseling
7. A program oriented to the school's community

A widely accepted goal of middle school education is a program which addresses all dimensions of growth during this period of human development. The interrelationships and interdependence of the physical, social, emotional, and intellectual realms are real. Each of these growth areas is vital to the development of fully functioning adults and, more immediately, to successful adjustment and school performance of the student during this period. The middle school program must be comprehensive.

Since a distinctive characteristic of middle school children is their differences in physical size, intellectual capacity, social adjustment, and emotional stability, it follows that the program must acknowledge these differences in planning. Each child must be perceived by school planners as unique in his or her passage through these developmental stages. The program must focus on the individual student, dealing with needs, interests, and rates of growth.

In conjunction with the above, the program in the middle school must individualize the learning process. Since each individual student is growing at his or her own innate rate of development, and since that rate of development in the four dimensions of concern is not parallel, the school's expectations for each student and the actual school performance of each student must be treated individually. If instruction for the middle school student is to be optimal in its impact, it must be directed to individual readiness and the capacity of the learner.

A practical means of individualizing the learning process, as distinct from individualizing instruction, is to tie learning activities directly to the needs and interests of the student. Because preadolescence is an age of extensive interest expansion, and because learning research in education is consistent in linking learner interest with retention, planners must attempt to make school experiences as relevant to the needs of the student as possible. Since the goals of middle school education are process-oriented, (skills, use of information) rather than product-oriented (mastery learning), student input into curriculum planning is both desirable and necessary.

The goal of comprehensive growth and development for the preadolescent suggests that middle school curriculums should do more to facilitate such personal growth through its everyday programs. Such programs, to maximize individual growth for each student, should be humane in nature, stress-free where possible, and should feature patterns of success for all students.

While school leaders have paid lip-service to humaness in education for a century in America, actions speak louder than words. Humane schools are places where it is accpetable to make mistakes, where free expression is valued, where exploration is perceived as essential, where learner input is seen as an asset to the learning process, where emphasis is placed on succeeding rather than failing, where students are given increasing amounts of responsibility for their own actions, and where, foremost, the individual is always more important than the institution or its standard programs.

Middle school programs which emphasize intensive guidance and counseling for all students reflects an awarensss of the critical affective dimensions of this period of development. Preadolescents, like children in early childhood, are in a formative stage of growth. The realignment of perceptions and values, the often strong dissonance between the goals and realities of social existence, and the continuous need to express and define such concerns to others about them suggests the need for an extraordinary guidance component in middle schools.

Finally, an important part of any middle school program is its relationship to the community about it. Not only are community resources valuable, but they also contribute greatly to the learning process in middle schools. Even more important is the fact that many of the problems and concerns of middle school students arise and are resolved outside the school. The degree of linkage between the middle school curriculum and community resources and agencies determines the quality of service the school can give to the specialized needs of its client, the student. The exact nature of this school-community relationship depends, of course, on the community in which the school resides.

These seven key elements, then, give structure to the middle school curriculum. They are sub-goals which shape activity. They characterize the uniqueness of middle school education and distinguish it from other existing forms of intermediate education. They define the scope of the school's aspirations to assist the preadolescent in his or her passage through this period of growth and development.

The ultimate design of any given middle school program will, of course, be shaped by socio-economic factors in the school environment such as budget, community attitudes toward education, student population, teacher talents, and administrative expertise. The implementation or development phase of establishing a middle school program is always subject to such restriction.

Still, the basic order of any middle school program should reflect the distinct concerns of the middle school movement. The school philosophy, its stated objectives, its theory of learning, and its instructional strategies all should combine to form a unique curricular design:

Philosophy. The school philosophy should be primarily concerned with the growth and development of each individual learner to maximum potential.

Goals. Should speak of broadly focused program of education oriented toward uninterrupted processes of growth rather than artificial "products" of an education.

Learning Theory. Should be directed toward individual learners, and focused on their needs in adjusting to immense change.

Instructional Strategy. Should build in the needs and interests of learners as natural sources of motivational energy by utilizing common denominators such as developmental tasks.

Educational programs in the middle school result from the identification of a particular philosophy, a set of priorities or obligations, ideas about the nature of the learning process in the classroom, and finally from emerging instructional strategies which reflect those concerns.

A Suggested Program Design

Since developmental tasks represent a set of needs common to **All** students in the middle school, and since they hold promise as one means of individualizing the school's program, it is possible to design learning experiences around such needs.

17

The developmental tasks confronted in preadolescence, outlined in the first chapter, can be grouped into five general areas of concern:

Academic adequacy
Social Awareness
Aesthetic Expansion
Self-Realization
Physical Development

These five global areas, collectively, could define the scope of curricular concern within the school's program as represented by this drawing:

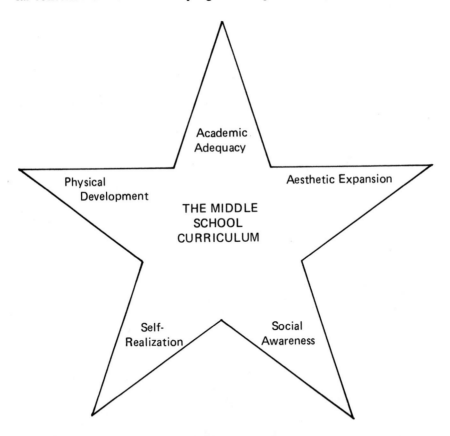

In a well-designed middle grades curriculum each of these dimensions of growth would be given parity. There should be no single dimension of development which dominates the structure of the program or the activities of the school. Each of these need areas, it is recognized, is interdependent with, and of equal importance to, the comprehensive development of the student in the middle grades.

Within each of these areas of focus, definite and unique learning objectives can be developed. These objectives are suggested to the planner by the tasks of growth, by the environmental conditions of the community, and by the nature of the population of learners. Below are listed sample goal statements and learning objectives for each of the five areas of focus:

Academic Adequacy

Preadolescence is a period of distinct expansion of intellectual capacities in the human being. Reflections of such expansion are the emergence of novel interests, a curiosity about adult roles, the first display of unusual academic talents, and a concern with meanings and values. If the learner is to receive maximum benefit as an individual from his school experience, a certain amount of academic achievement is demanded. Academic adequacy results from the mastery of certain basal knowledge, the development of some communication and computational skills, and the sharpening of various academic attitudes.

Objectives

1. To develop a base of information sources.
2. To master computational skills and understand the need for them.
3. To develop the ability to communicate ideas and feelings by developing skills in reading, listening, speaking, and writing.
4. To develop the ability to identify and apply skills necessary in problem solving situations.
5. To develop disciplined and logical thought processes.
6. To develop the ability to carefully examine and criticize information.
7. To develop and promote one's intellectual curiosity.
8. To develop an appreciation for processes that will stimulate independent and continued learning.

Social Awareness

Social changes during the preadolescent period are dramatic and stressful. Opposite sex relationships become critical, peer group acceptance important, the assumption of adultlike roles desirable, and the achievement of status a paramount concern. All students have a need to be aware of and responsive to the structure and functions of the society.

Such an awareness is best gained by a study of the society about the student. An understanding of roles, relationships and responsibilities open to individuals will assist in making such changes less stressful.

19

Objectives
1. To understand the human social network called society and its historical evolution.
2. To explore and understand the interdependence of individuals in our societal network.
3. To analyze the social values which underlie our social institutions.
4. To evaluate social roles in society in terms of age, sex, race, religion, and philosophy.
5. To explore sources of social conflict through discussion and encounter with other individuals.
6. To evelute the works of various community agencies in promoting social cohesiveness.
7. To understand the rewards, problems, and requirements of careers available to students.
8. To evaluate the freedoms and responsibilities inherent in a Democracy.
9. To analyze the interdependence of all nations and people.

Aesthetic Expansion

During the preadolescent years, latent talents and interests unfold briefly while the learner is realigning his perceptions and values and understandings of the surrounding world. Programs in the middle grades, capitalizing on the new openness, can assist the learner in preparing for a richer, fuller adulthood.

Such an expansion of aesthetic capacities calls for a broadening of the learners understanding of man's aesthetic endeavors, a face-to-face introduction to aesthetic experiences, and the development of an appreciation for the aesthetic dimensions of living.

Objectives
1. To develop a basic source of knowledge about the aesthetic dimensions of social existence.
. 2. To stimulate the student's interface with aesthetic experiences.
3. To develop and promote latent aesthetic talents of all pupils.
4. To assist students in the discovery and development of leisure time activities.
5. To promote an understanding and appreciation of the aesthetic dimensions of human existence.
6. To facilitate an understanding of the commonality of aesthetic expression among all of the world's peoples.

Self-Realization

Preadolescence is a period of intense introspection and interest in **Self**. While this invisible "price Tag" is often defined by peers and significant adults, self-realization is still a function of perception and experience. School programs can promote flexible and positive self-concepts.

Learners who more fully explore their own strengths and weaknesses, who relate those conditions to others about them, and who can be accepting of themselves will be more productive and supportive citizens.

Objectives

1. To identify personal strengths and shortcomings in physical, social, and academic areas.
2. To develop an understanding of social norms and values held by society.
3. To develop the capacity to analyze and solve personal problems.
4. To accept oneself in the present and strive for self-improvement through future planning.

Physical Development

During the preadolescent period the body is undergoing major changes. There are significant alterations of bone and muscle tissue, and changes in body chemistry are causing observable changes to external features of the preadolescent. Awkwardness, restlessness, and abundant energy make the student an unlikely candidate for the passive reception of knowledge. Gaining information about and accepting one's physical self is an area of concern. Developing oneself to maximum potential and to make health a regular part of one's life is a goal.

Objectives

1. To have a familiarity with the mechanics and physical processes of the human body.
2. To understand the nutritional needs of the body.
3. To gain a working knowlege of one's sexual self in terms of development past, present, future.
4. To develop a knowledge of personal hygiene.
5. To gain an acceptance of one's physical self in terms of body image and physical potential.
6. To develop oneself to this physical potential of fitness through an exercise program individually suited to the learners needs.
7. To develop and pursue ones physical interests through participation in a variety of recreational sports and activities.

While educational planners in the middle school would select their own goal areas and objectives according to the needs of their learners and the other kinds of educational opportunities available to students in the community, a comprehensive and balanced program is desired.

21

The curriculum in the middle grades, the design of the school's programs, represents society's intersection with the growth and development patterns of its future citizens. As such, that intersection cannot be neutral in character. The school curriculum is, through its design, society's arrangement to shape the growth and development of individuals into desirable patterns. Whether the society, through its schools and teachers, wishes to control the outcome of growth or trusts a natural outcome, is mirrored in the type of activities engaged in by the student.

While the curriculum of the middle school has traditionally been more open-ended than other levels of schooling, it must be recognized that structure and direction are essential in the middle grades. A program which encourages a loss of talent, deviant social behavior, or exclusion from the intellectual mainstream of society is counterproductive.

It is apparent that an educational program in the middle school cannot be captured by compartmentalized subject matter, or by the historic dominance of the didactic teaching methodologies. Rather, it seems logical that such a student-focused program must build in curricular flexibility, gravitate toward interest-centered resources units, and begin to perceive education as a process rather than a product. The selection of the means of delivery, however, should be the result of a thorough analysis of the desired goals of education in the middle grades. Further treatment of program construction is found in chapter four.

Chapter Summary

The design of a program of education in the middle school is drawn from a number of planning considerations: an educational philosophy, distinctive elements or priorities of the program, a theory and strategy of instruction, local conditions and resources, and a way of ordering learning opportunities.

The middle school design is constructed around the needs of preadolescents and features an individualized learning program which is characterized by humaneness and relevance. The learning activities in the middle school focus on needs common to all learners. Five major areas of focus, with objectives, represent the author's suggested program organizer. The coordination of all planning considerations is essential to program success.

SUGGESTED READING

Barnes, D. "Your Middle School Must Have a Revised Program." *Educational Leadership,* December, 1973.

Grambs, J. *"The Junior High School We Need."* Association for Supervision and Curriculum Development, 1961.

Eichhorn, Donald H. "Middle School Organization: A New Dimension." *Theory into Practice* XLVI, 2, 67-73, October, 1971.

Merritt, Daniel L. "Middle School: Organization for Learning." *Middle School Journal,* V, 5, Winter, 1974.

NOTES

3

PLANNING CONSIDERATIONS
IN THE DEVELOPMENT
OF MIDDLE SCHOOLS

The curriculum of the middle school, with its concern for the special needs of preadolescents, with its comprehensive definition of education, with its promotion of continuity in learning and development, is more than a series of catch phrases and educational innovations. The middle school curriculum is, in fact, a highly complex plan for educating a special learner. Due to the complexity of the educational design, successful implementation of the program calls for a significant degree of advanced planning.

Many understandings and decisions are necessary to initiate and promote the middle school concept. The type and size of the community, the amount of funding, the availability of facilities, the type and quality of materials and equipment, and the availability and resourcefulness of trained personnel are but a few of the primary concerns.

In assisting a number of middle schools during the establishment stage, the author has noted that planning often determines the fine line between success and failure. Such planning is necessary at the district, school, and classroom level if the program of the middle school is to succeed. This chapter seeks to provide guidelines which will assist middle schools in avoiding problems which can be overcome by planning.

District Level Planning

As often as not, middle schools come into being because dedicated intermediate educators are seeking a better way to serve their students. If programs originate at the school level, however, their development is sometimes delayed by a lack of planning at the school district level. The system which constructs a building without understanding the middle school concept, for instance, is going to handicap the program somewhere in the future. District level planning must be conducted if the middle school concept is to succeed in one of its schools.

It is the further observation of the author that the *sequence* of district level planning is particularly important to the smooth implementation of programs. The following district level planning steps, in sequence, are recommended in the establishment of a middle school.

25

Analysis. **The middle school should arise from need.**

While it is ideal to hope that school systems and communities will proceed through value clarification processes which reveal the logic of the middle school design, it is hoped that programs will be initiated based on what is known about their students. Overcrowding, integration, or building availability are poor reasons for choosing the concept.

An important point in making such an analysis is not to allow the search to be focused only on problems. It should also be projective in nature; what kind of an educational experience do we want for students during this period of development?

Involvement. **Preliminary investigations of the middle school should involve all parties with vested interests in intermediate education.**

A step often taken in planning the middle school is to explore the concept without involving those who will be most directly affected by its activation: students, teachers, parents, and the community. At a superficial level, the elimination of this stage will probably lead to future confrontations over both programs and policy (interscholastic athletics, social events, grading policies, community-based learning). More important from the planning standpoint, however, is the dedication and support that will be needed to put such a program into practice in the first place. **The middle school cannot be implemented and maintained unless it is believed in by those involved.**

Of the above mentioned constituencies, particular attention must be given to the community in which the middle school will reside. Not being used to education jargon, and unfamiliar with national trends in educational programs, many citizens will resist the middle school because of misunderstandings about the academic nature of the program and the necessary organizational arrangements. Without a clear understanding of the rationale of the program and the reason for these arrangements, community suspicion and resistance will be high.

Involvement of community members representing all segments of the population in the initial analysis of student needs, in the investigation of the middle school concept, in the drafting of documents, and in the planning of implementation stages will build in a means of communicating with the community-at-large at later times.

Commitment. **Philophical commitments to the middle school definition of education should be secured prior to activating the program.**

This book has repeatedly underscored the necessity of understanding and accepting the middle school's philosophic position on education as a prerequisite for successful implementation of such a program. **An understanding or lack of understanding of the middle school concept rep-**

resents the largest potential stumbling block to successful implementation. Without such understanding and a basic philosophic acceptance of the middle school concept, there can be no substantial rationale for practices and programs found in the middle school.

It is important to note that this understanding and acceptance must go beyond school board approval and superintendent acquiescence—though both of the above are important. Such an understanding and commitment must be held by the building principal, the involved teachers, and the majority of the parents of involved students.

Funding. **Appropriate monies must be earmarked for activation of the plan.**

It is an observable phenomena in American education that finance is the "fuel" of progress. Few major innovations of the past twenty years, middle schools being a notable exception, have really succeeded without substantial financial support.

While it is not impossible for a building faculty to implement the middle school concept with sheer dedication, two simple facts about middle schools are worth noting: **Middle schools are a more complex form of education than traditional programs and middle schools therefore require more energy and money to operate.**

Every deviation from standardized patterns of educating, such as the uniform textbooks, the classroom-confined learning experience, and the single-dimension instruction, will require effort and expense. As school districts do commit themselves to the middle school concept, a pledge equal to their commitment for financing building conversion, materials acquisition, staff development and so forth is called for.

Resources. **Resources commensurate with the task must be allocated.**

One of the common pitfalls in establishment of middle schools is to assume that they can operate on the same resource base as the traditional intermediate school. To rely on teacher-made materials exclusively, to overlook a consumable materials budget, to fail to allocate materials to build up the instructional resource center, to make no provision for off-campus experiences and so forth is to doom in advance the programs of the middle school. **Middle schools, if properly operated, require substantial resources for instruction.**

Personnel. **There must be an attempt to staff middle schools with dedicated and enthusiastic teachers.**

There are several appropriate comments to note regarding the selection, training and use of middle school staff. The middle school will be only as effective as its personnel are in succeeding at new roles. With only several colleges in the nation training teachers and staff members exclusively for middle school positions, most teachers and support personnel will enter the middle school from other more traditional educational designs. Such persons, regardless of their belief in and allegiance to the middle school philosophy of educating, will need special assistance in adjusting to their new roles. **It can be expected that the middle school staff will need extensive assistance in assuming new roles.**

A problem witnessed in many school districts is that middle school teacher behaviors are prone to return to traditional patterns if sufficient support isn't maintained. Many middle schools open under the so-called Hawthone Effect,* and with such a condition teacher enthusiasm and energy is understandably high. However, as program development slows or resource bases erode with the gradual lessening of attention, it isn't unusual for old patterns of teacher-pupil interaction and learning to creep in. Such a condition would warn against a one-shot summer treatment for the middle school staff and would call for long-term and systematic training opportunities.

Detailed Planning. **Prior to the development of a middle school it is essential that detailed planning be conducted.**

From an administrative/organizational perspective, it is crucial that schools conduct detailed planning in order to smoothly implement the middle school concept. The past experience of many middle schools suggests that a "broken front" approach to this concept does not work. The middle school concept does not easily emerge because there are prerequisites for inplementation. There must be an understanding of objectives; there must be a commitment to this definition of educating; there must be an involvement of those who support the school; there must be money and resources to implement it's components; there must be personnel capable of and willing to assume the required roles. **The time frame for opening a middle school must consider the magnitude of the process proposed.**

While the amount of preparation time required to open a real middle school is dependent upon environmental conditions in the community, a minimum period appears to be eighteen to twenty-four months. This estimate is based on several definable steps of planning:

1. Awareness and study phases.
2. Educating community and gaining commitments.
3. Budgeting for development.
4. Selection of staff, site.

*A term coming from the Hawthone Studies in which workers were found to be more productive regardless of work conditions if they received sufficient attention as being special.

5. Construction of detailed implementation plan.
6. Intensive training of staff.
7. Development of curriculum.
8. Construction or conversion of site.
9. Opening of middle school.

It is recognized that in some communities and school districts it would be possible to accomplish the above steps in six months or less due to central office organization and support from the community leaders. The experience of many middle schools, though, would suggest that to hasten through steps 2, 6, and 7, or to proceed with step 8 prior to step 7 leads to significant problems later on. **Eroding community support, an ill-prepared staff, a superficially constructed curriculum, and a dysfunctional site all are common causes of middle school failure.**

Determining the Odds for Success

Not all communities are ready for a middle school. As with its predecessor, the junior high school, the middle school has achieved tremendous numerical growth in a relatively short period of time. The rush of this "bandwagon" effect has caused many communities to plan and construct middle schools without due consideration of the implications of their actions. When the true nature of the middle school program is first revealed to parents and to teachers not involved in decision making, there can be misunderstandings and conflict.

The implementation of educational change is always a relatively unpredictable phenomena due to the immense number of variables involved. One research project sponsored by the State of Florida and directed by the author sought, through study and on-site observation, to identify those crucial variables which indicate the probability of an educational innovation being accepted at the building level. While the profile on the next page in no way promises success for those attempting to open a middle school, it can provide a rough pattern for study. Such a device is also helpful in directing energies to increase the changes of successful implementation.

Building Level Planning

Beyond district level planning for middle school programs is the preparation at the building level. If substantial and lasting curriculum change is to occur in schools, the planning of such change must be both comprehensive and coordinated. Existing literature on change in school environments suggests that curricular alterations of school programs is both complex and difficult to control. It appears that such changes dealing with programs are

29

Educational Innovations
Probability Chart

High Risk ← →Lower Risk

Source of Innovation	Superimposed from outside	Outside agent brought in	Developed internally with aid	External idea modified	Locally conceived, developed, implemented
Impact of Innovation	Challenges sacrosanct beliefs	Calls for major value shifts	Requires substantial change	Modifies existing values or programs	Does not substantially alter existing values, beliefs or programs
Official Support	Official leaders active opposition	Officials on record as opposing	Officials uncommitted	Officials voice support of change	Enthusiastically supported by the official leaders
Planning of Innovation	Completely external	Most planning external	Planning processes balanced	Most of planning done locally	All planning for change done on local site
Means of Adoption	By superiors	By local leaders	By Reps	By most of the clients	By group concensus
History of Change	History of failures	No accurate records on	Some success with innovation	A history of successful innovations	Known as school where things regularly succeed
Possibility of Revision	No turning back	Final evaluation before committee	Periodic evaluations	Possibility of abandoning at conclusion	Possible to abort the effort at any time
Role of Teachers	Largely bypassed	Minor role	Regular role in implementing	Heavy role in implementation	Primary actor in the classroom effort
Teacher Expectation	Fatalistic	Feel little chance	Are willing to give a try	Confident of success	Wildly enthusiastic about chance of success
Work Load Measure	Substantially increased	Heavier but rewarding	Slightly increased	Unchanged	Work load lessened by the innovation
Threat Measure	Definitely threatens some clients	Probably threatening to some	Mild threat resulting from the change	Very remote threat to some	Does not threaten the security or autonomy
Community Factor	Hostile to innovations	Suspicious and uninformed	Indifferent	Ready for a change	Wholeheartedly supports the school

Shade the response in each category which most accurately reflects the condition surrounding the implementation of the middle school. If the "profile" of your school is predominately in the high risk side of the matrix, substantial work must be done to prepare your school for change.

30

rarely isolates and comprise, intentionally or otherwise, a series of inter-related and interdependent events. The challenge to building level planners is to develop a comprehensive monitoring device to observe and direct the numerous on-going changes. One such "building blueprint" is the developmental staging concept.

Developmental staging is basically a construct using a form of "discrepancy analysis." It consists of outlining anticipated change steps in program development which are intermediate conditions between what currently exists and what is desired. In a sense, developmental staging attempts to break down the sometimes enormous gaps between the "real" and "ideal" while at the same time displaying the comprehensive nature of the change being planned.

The utility of the "staging" concept to promote desired curricular change is dependent upon several essential conditions. First, it is assumed that some sort of philosophical consensus is present among those engaged in the change process so that terminal goals can be described and progress toward those goals accurately assessed. Stated simply, it is impossible to construct a chart of progression toward desired goals in the middle school program if such ends are not clearly identified and agreed upon.

Second, it is vital that the staging plans leading toward desired goals begin with an accurate portrait of present realities. A staff must use its best judgment to distinguish between educational intentions and day-to-day practices. Often times the only accurate means of testing such potential discrepancies is to view the condition or practice through the eyes of a single randomly-selected middle school student. What is read, what is desired?

Finally, the use of developmental staging should always be preceded by an acceptance of the fact that lasting change of a curricular nature is almost always a tedious process. A predisposition toward patience and a longview of progress will assist a staff in a thoughtful identification of stages of progress.

Continuums of Progress

In global reorientations of school programs, such as in the design of a middle school, monitoring categories of school change can provide more accurate indicators of progress toward desired ends. In one southern city, for instance, a planning team identified fourteen areas in which they felt progress should be monitored:

Moving From

1. *Philosophy*

   A written document on file in the school office, defining the school

Moving Toward

   An active, working philosophy which is known by all teachers and in terms of knowledge areas and administrative concerns.

which serves as the basis of day-to-day decision making. Defines the school in terms of expected learner growth.

2. *School Plant*

Using only standard classroom spaces for instructional purposes.

Encompassing varied learning environments, using all available building spaces for instructional purposes (school yard, corridors).

3. *Staffing Patterns*

Isolated teachers in self-contained classes.

Teachers grouped in cooperative arrangements, dealing with large numbers of learners collectively. Planning time and home-base teaching function built in organizationally.

4. *Instructional Materials*

Classrooms dominated by a basic grade-level text. Libraries usually study halls for large class groups.

Diversified learning materials within any given classroom setting; "something for everybody." Multiple texts, supplemental software, integrated and cross-subject materials. Heavy use of multimedia learning resource centers for independent exploration.

5. *Organization of Students*

Basic pattern of one teacher and thirty students in standardized room spaces. Students in same sized groups all day.

Greater variability in the sizes of learning groups ranging from individualized study to large group (120 students) instruction. Grouped according to the objective of the instruction.

6. *Teaching Strategies*

Variety of approaches found but most classes dominated by lecture, single text, question-answer format.

Greater variety of patterns of teacher-pupil interchange. Teaming when advantageous, greater use of media, possible peer teaching, counseling, more hands-on experiences.

7. *Role of the Teacher*

Defined in terms of subject(s) taught. Teacher perceived as source of knowledge and responsible for order.

Greater concern with students. A planned teacher-counselor role. More group work (projects, issues). Teacher role an organizer, facilitator of learning experiences.

Teacher monitoring "contracts" with students. Shared responsibility for order.

8. *Role of Student*

Passive recipient of knowledge. Most instruction paced to group. A reactive posture.

Greater input and chance for expression. Involved in planning. Goal to become self-directed. Emphasis on self-conduct and "success." Use of contracts for student goal setting.

9. *Role of Parents*

Limited access to the schools. Few parents involved at meaningful level. Involvement in only administrative concerns.

Greater involvement of all parents in school activities. Opportunities for more direct involvement in instructional roles in classroom and curriculum planning. Greater flow of information to parents about school objectives and program.

10. *Role of Community*

Limited interface with schools. Some strong foundational ties with social services in the city.

School becoming more outwardly oriented; seeing the community as a learning environment and source of instructional resources. Systematizing the connections with social services in the community.

11. *School Rules and Regulations*

High degree of regimentation through rules and regulation. Little student input into process. High degree of student dependence on adults for direction.

Greater involvement of students in the design of regulatory policies. Identifying the really essential rules . . . aiming toward minimum acceptable level of control. Goal to foster increased student independence and self-control.

12. *Discipline*

Reactive pattern of discipline, ranging from admonishment and parent conferences to paddling and expulsion.

Designing an active program to deter potential disciplinary problems. Greater involvement of pupils in process. Insured degrees or success for all students, seeking to curtail frustration and boredom.

13. *Reporting of Student Progress*

Letter grades assigned, concern with only narrowly defined academic progress.

Striving for varied student evaluation using a more descriptive medium (conferences, student

| 14. *Staff Development* | folders, etc.). Focused on all dimensions of student growth. |
| Global, not closely tied to building level needs of teachers and students. | Designed to attack building level problems identified by teachers and students. Development of a monitoring process to measure achievement of predetermined goals. |

Taking the above areas of concern for middle school development, and grouping them under headings such as the school environment, participant roles, instructional arrangements, and administrative conditions will allow middle school planners to begin to see connected "areas" of concern.

In the model of developmental staging provided herein, areas within each of the four large categories are followed through five major stages of development. Stage one in each of the categories describes in a few words the realities of present conditions. Stage two reflects an awareness of the directions of change and possibly some "tinkering" with the status quo. Stage three is generally an experimentation stage during which the desired changes are auditioned. Stage four represents an adoption stage during which the change is institutionalized or supported by administrative acts. Stage five is a brief description of the ideal condition or stage being pursued.

Regardless of the nature of the change or the value system such change represents or reflects, it is crucial that a description of the stages be derived from the statement of purpose or philosophy. Such "guidance" will promote consistency among the stages and therefore support continuous progress toward the desired changes.

The present condition of the school described below (stage 1) is not unlike that of many schools across the nation. There is either no philosophic statement of purposes or such a statement is left over from the last accreditation visit and remains locked in the principal's desk drawer.

The environment of the school shows "learning" occurring only in the standard classroom spaces, and those spaces are characterized by meager materials. There is little or no interchange between the school and the immediate neighborhood and community about it.

Roles at the school are highly traditional. The principal is the "boss," the broker of rights and favors, the enforcer of rules. Teachers represent units of subject matter specialization. Students are passive and without individual academic identity.*

The instructional organization of the school causes the teachers to be

*Wiles, J. W. Developmental Staging—in pursuit of comprehensive curriculum planning. *Middle School Journal,* Vol. vi, number 1. Spring 1975.

cut off and isolated from each other. Teaching is chiefly by lecture method, and the instructional team is receiving random doses of "help" from periodic district staff development efforts.

Administrative conditions find students regimented for convenience and economy. Student progress is reported in abbreviated letter or number symbols in five or six arbitrarily selected areas of growth. The school is dominated by a plethora of rules—rules for any and all occasions—and by a reactive and repetitive program of discipline.

The ideal or desired condition (stage 5), on the other hand, represents a very different portrait for the developing middle school. This school aspires to a tailor-made learning environment. This wish for a logical allocation of available resources to serve educational ends, individualized curricular opportunities for students, and programmatic ties to the potential riches of the community beyond its walls.

The desired roles for this transitional middle school would feature involved and self-reliant students, facilitating and creative teachers, and supportive administrators who themselves are instructional leaders within the building.

The desired instructional program would have organizational arrangements which reflect the intentions of the curricular components. There would be a variety of instructional patterns present at any given moment, and problems would be resolved with the aid of specific staff development assistance.

Administrative conditions, ideally, would be supportive of the curricular program, and therefore flexible to change as program focus and intentions change. Report of student progress would be comprehensive, individualized and descriptive. Rules and regulations would be minimal. Discipline, when needed, would be efficient and effective in changing behavior.

The usefulness of the developmental staging concept in the planning of a middle school program is multi-faceted. Such a technique can provide a ready profile of a school and its educational program and display areas of concern. Using a staged format, discrepancies, inconsistencies, and severe problem areas can be identified and confronted.

Developmental staging also serves as a master blueprint for comprehensive change and, where stages are defined and described in behavioral terms, a tool for periodic evaluation. As a display of reality and a picture of progress, it can serve as a medium for in-house communication.

Most important for emerging middle schools, however, is the usefulness of the staging concept in overcoming feelings of "powerlessness." Such feelings result from being overwhelmed by the many dimensions of the change process in school environments. In dealing with the sometimes wide gulf between real conditions and ideal conditions, those involved in plan-

	Present Condition	Awareness Stage	Experimentation Stage	Adoption Stage	Desired Condition
	Stage 1	Stage 2	Stage 3	Stage 4	Stage 5
The School Philosophy	Either no formal statement or a written document on file in the school office.	School staff share beliefs, look for consensus, restate philosophy and objectives in terms of expected behavior.	Staff begins use of goals as guide to evaluating school practices. Begin to involve students and community in planning.	Philosophy and goals used to shape the program. Formal mechanism established to monitor program and decision making.	Philosophy a living document. Guides daily decisions. The program a tool for achieving desired educational ends.

The Learning Environment

	Present Condition	Awareness Stage	Experimentation Stage	Adoption Stage	Desired Condition
	Stage 1	Stage 2	Stage 3	Stage 4	Stage 5
Use of the Building	Only uniform instructional spaces. Little use of the building spaces for educational purposes.	Some deviation from traditional space utilization (classroom learning center). Possibly a complete demonstration class for bright ideas.	Limited building conversion (knock out walls). Begin to identify unused spaces. Planning for large learning spaces.	Development of a comprehensive plan for use of grounds and building. Total remodeling of spaces.	Tailor-made learning environment—all spaces used to educate. Building facilitates the learning intention.
Use of Materials	Classrooms are dominated by a grade-level text. Library with a limited offering. Used as a study hall for large groups.	Use of multi-level texts within classroom. Materials selected after an analysis of student achievement levels. Supplemental resources made available to students.	Diverse materials developed for the students. Resource centers established. Cross-discipline selection of materials. More multi-media used. Some independent study.	Materials purchasing policies realigned. Common learning areas established as resource centers. More self-directed study built in.	Diversified materials. Something for each student. Integrated subject materials. Portable curriculum units (on carts). Heavy multi-media. Active learning centers.
Use of Community	Little or no access to school. Information about programs scanty. Trust low.	Some school program ties to community. Token access via PTA and media. School perceived as island in neighborhood.	Preliminary uses of community as learning environment. Identification of nearby resources. Use of building for community functions.	Regular interchange between school and community. Systematic communication. A network of services and resources established.	School programs outwardly oriented. Community seen as a teaching resource. Systematic ties with services and resources around school.

Instructional Organization

Staffing Patterns	Building teachers isolated in self-contained class-rooms. Little or no lateral communication or planning present.	Limited sharing of re-sources. Some division of labor and small-scale cooperation in teaching. Informal communication about student progress.	Regular cooperative planning sessions. Some curricular integration via themes. Students rotate through subject areas. Problems of cooperation identified.	Interdepartmental organization. Use of common planning time. Administrative support such as in scheduling. Use of philosophy as curricular decision-making criteria.
				Teaching staff a "team" working toward common ends. Staff patterns reflect instructional intentions. Administration in support of curricular design. Coursework integrated for students.
Teaching Strategy	Some variety but lecture and teacher-dominated Q-A session the norm. Homework used to promote day-to-day continuity.	Observation of other teaching models. Skill development via workshops. An identification of staff strengths and weaknesses. Some new patterns.	Building level experiments by willing staff members. "Modeling" of ideas. On-site consultant help made available for skill development.	School day divided according to the teaching strategy employed. Faculty evaluation of the effectiveness of new ways after a trial period.
				Great variety of methods used in teaching, uses of media, dealing with students. The curricular plans determine strategy.
Staff Development	Staff development is global, rarely used to attack local needs and problems. Occurs as needed.	Staff identifies in-service needs and priorities. Philosophy assists in this process. Local staff skills and strengths are recognized.	Staff development re-aligned to serve needs of teachers. Opportunities for personal growth are made available.	Formal procedures for directing staff development to needs established. Staff development seen as problem-solving mechanism.
				Staff development an on-going process using available resources. An attempt to close theory-practice gaps.

Administrative Conditions

	Present Condition Stage 1	Awareness Stage Stage 2	Experimentation Stage Stage 3	Adoption Stage Stage 4	Desired Condition Stage 5
Organization of Student	Uniform patterns. One teacher, 30 students in six rows of five in each row in each period of each school day.	Understanding that organization of students should match curricular intentions. Some initial variation of group sizes in classroom.	Limited organization to facilitate the grouping of the students. Begin use of aides and parents to increase organizational flexibility.	Full administrative support for a reorganization of students. Building restructed where necessary. An increase in planning for effectiveness.	Group sizes vary according to the activity planned. Full support given to eliminate any problem areas.
Report of Student Progress	"Progress" is defined narrowly. Letter grades or simple numerals represent student learning in the subject areas.	Recognition of broader growth goals for students. Use of philosophy to evaluate the existing practices.	Experimentation with supplemental reporting procedures. Involvement of student and parents in the process.	Development of a diverse and comprehensive reporting procedure for student progress.	Descriptive medium used to monitor individual student progress. Broadly focused evaluation. Team of teacher, student, and parents involved.
Rules and Regulations	High degree of regimentation. Many rules, most inherited over the years. The emphasis on the enforcement and on control.	Staff and students identify essential rules. Regulations matched against the school philosophy.	Rules and regulations streamlined. Used as a teaching device about life outside of school. Increased student self-control.	Greater use of student and staff input into the regulation of the school environment. Rewards built-in for desirable performance.	Moving toward minimal regulation and an increased student self-control. Regulations a positive teaching device.
Discipline	Reactive pattern ranging from verbal admonishment to paddling and expulsion. Reoccurring offenders.	Staff analysis of school policies. Shift of emphasis to causes of the problems. Some brainstorming of possible solutions.	Establishment of a hierarchy of discipline activity. Begin implementing preventive strategies.	Design of curriculum programs to deter discipline problems. High intensity program for regular offenders.	Program of the school eliminates most sources of discipline problems. The procedure for residual problems clear to all.

Roles of Participants

Student Roles	Passive recipient of knowledge. Instruction is geared to average student. Reactive communication with the teacher.	Investigation of new student roles by teacher. Limited hierarchy of trust established in the classroom. Needs and interests of student investigated.	Groundrules for increased student independence set. Student involvement in planning. Role of student connected to philosophy of the school.	Periodic staff review of student roles. Roles linked to school-wide rules and regulations. Philosophy guides role possibilities.	Students involved in planning and conducting the program. Increased independence *and* responsibility. Use of "contracts" to maintain new understandings.
Teacher Roles	Defined by the subjects taught. Perceived as the source of all knowledge. Other roles peripheral.	Perceiving roles suggested by the philosophy. Roles accepted at verbal level. Limited experimentation with new roles.	Investigation of new roles—trying on new relationship. Goal-setting for individual teacher. Skill development through in-service.	Administrative reorganization for role support. A sharpened planning and action skills needed to serve the student according to the philosophy.	Teacher role is defined by student needs. Teacher the organizer of the learning activities. Teacher talents used more effectively.
Principal Roles	Solely responsible for school operation. The "boss". Enforcer of all rules. The linkage to all outside information and resources.	Awareness of role limitations. An awareness of real leadership potential. A setting of role priorities.	Limited sharing of decision-making in area of curriculum. Limited joint planning with the faculty. Review of existing policy according to the philosophy.	Role perception changes to manager of resources. Emphasis on development (active) rather than on order (static). Increase in curriculum leadership functions.	An instructional leader. Administrative acts support the curriculum program. Philosophy guiding decision-making. Built-in monitoring system for evaluating building level progress.

ning and development of the middle school can "witness" progress in the many continuums and experience the "pace" or momentum of the changes occurring.

The ends to be pursued, the categories to be monitored, and the proofs of progress in stages should be all developed internally by those persons involved in planning and implementing the middle school. Developmental staging as outlined above is a useful concept in serving as a curricular blueprint for development.

It should be noted in passing that the staging concept outlined here can be valuably linked with management devices, such as PERT/CPM, to give an even clearer picture of progress toward desired ends. It is felt that the development of the middle school concept, without such an effort to perceive and control the complexities of change, can cause the permanent division of theory and practice, thereby undermining the credibility of middle school potential.

Classroom Level

In preparing for the middle school within a building, at the classroom or instructional level, planners must be concerned with roles of the instructional staff, the preparation of instructional staff members, and the arrangements which must be made to enable teaching in the middle school to be effective.

Due to the intentions of the middle school program, the instructional component must be staffed by persons who are both enthusiastic and flexible. Since middle school learning focuses on students rather than predetermined bodies of subject matter, there is a continuous need for high degrees of communication, coordinated planning, and resource sharing among those in instructional roles. In short, the middle school design logically calls for interdisciplinary approaches to teaching.

Interdisciplinary approaches are simply one way to organize the middle school for instructional strength. This approach to teaching is compatible with middle school goals such as individualizing instruction, personalizing classroom interaction, and building in flexibility. Interdisciplinary teaching tends to free middle school teachers for creative instruction. Interdisciplinary arrangements allow for multiple-sized instructional groups, better communication among both teachers and students, better utilization of staff talents and expertise, and more efficient time and resource management.

Most important from the instructional standpoint, however, is that interdisciplinary teaching patterns cause the necessary involvement of the teacher in the learning process itself. The consequence of such an involvement is that the entire instructional staff tends to grow and develop along with students.

Instructional teams in middle schools tend to evolve through at least five stages as they develop into fully functioning units:

Stage 1. Teams are formed and exist in name only. Teachers are either still acting in a self-contained manner or are closely aligned in a social network. Administrative arrangements to facilitate the team development, such as released planning time, are nonexistent.

Stage 2. With the formation of teams, administrative support needs are recognized and built in. Teachers begin planning on a regular basis, but primarily for coordination of events. Subjects are still treated independently and usually follow one another in blocks of time.

Stage 3. Considerably greater cooperative arrangements begin to emerge among team members. Some work between subjects and some activities as extracurricular to the basic subject areas. Planning shows initial signs of imagination.

Stage 4. The majority of teaching in the team now along thematic lines. Old subject disciplines barely visible. Planning and communication improved and concern is with cooperation rather than coordination. Still perceiving team as group of teachers within a building.

Stage 5. Team cohesion very tight. Planning and communication feedback on-going. Students and other support personnel involved in planning and evaluation sessions. Activities and resource use spilling out of the building into the surrounding community and environment.

These five stages of team development indicate some areas where planning for instructional growth is necessary. Teachers must be able to communicate, cooperate, focus on areas of commonality, be concerned with student growth rather than subject matter mastery, and be prepared to work hard to produce a successful program for the students assigned to their teams.

In addition to the "teaching" staff in middle schools, there are other staff members who must be prepared to actively contribute to the instructional program. The roles of classroom teachers, such as guiding students in the understanding and application of information, being perceptive to student needs and interests, and providing challenge to each student to excel to his or her capacity, must be shared by other staff persons in the school.

These other persons form the "support team" in the middle school and they, too, must be prepared to contribute to the instructional process. Examples of this support team are:

Media/Materials Specialists
Guidance Services Specialists
Physical Development Specialists
Administrative Specialists

The Materials/Media Specialist

In the middle grades there is need for a specialist who is knowledgable about instructional resources and good at getting such information to the classroom teacher. Because teachers in the middle grades are constantly seeking new ideas and assistance in their attempt to individualize the learning process, most schools can no longer afford a mere cataloger or custodian of materials.

The materials/media specialist must become a learning diagnostician in an attempt to help match individual student needs with possible learning mediums. This person must also be skilled at setting up or delivering useful materials for classroom learning units. This specialist must regularly work closely with students, teachers, and the community to provide appropriate resources. The role of such a specialist might be defined thusly:

- Participating as a partner in curriculum development efforts.
- Keeping teachers informed of new and existing resources.
- Maintaining communication with outside instructional resource pools.
- Participating as a member of planning and teaching teams.
- Teaching students in the use of bibliographic tools in subject areas.
- Maintaining lines of communication with the community.

The Guidance Services Specialist

The guidance element in the middle grades is essential to the "total growth and development" concept of intermediate education. Guidance service specialists, be they counselors, advisors, teacher-counselors, parent volunteers, or professionals from related psychological services, make an especially valuable contribution in the social-emotional dimensions of student development. The work of these specialists should be coordinated with the classroom activities of regular teachers.

Because the average student load for each trained counselor in many intermediate schools exceeds 1:450, optimal use of such a resource person may come from activities other than simply interacting with students. Other roles which might be carried by such a support person are:

- The design and coordination of a comprehensive guidance program including components dealing with student appraisal, prescription and reference, and general information services.
- Training and working with teachers in fundamental guidance and counseling techniques to be used in classroom settings.
- Coordinating effective building communication about individual student needs, interests, abilities, and problems.
- Serving as liason to outside guidance components and related community services such as physicians, health units, employment services, and youth action agencies.

Physical Development Specialist

It would be shortsighted to perceive the role of the physical development specialist as simply an adult concerned with physical fitness through bodily exercise. A more comprehensive approach to such services is called for.

In addition to physical fitness, such a specialist might be concerned with basic health and sex education, and recreational opportunity. Special provisions would be made for the handicapped, the restricted, the underdeveloped student, and for those with a pronounced interest in physical education.

Roles of the physical development specialist might include:

- Working with regular teachers to develop an overall growth and development program for the middle grades.
- Assuming a coordinating role for interdisciplinary efforts necessary to implement a comprehensive physical development program.
- Assume the role of trainer of teachers in raising the level of awareness of physical problems and concerns of the preadolescent, and in suggesting programs which would promote positive growth.
- Serving as a resource person and link to outside resources in the areas of health and physical development.

Administrative Specialist

A final group of specialists within the intermediate school that contribute to instructional programs are those dealing with administrative matters. These persons organize, coordinate, and facilitate the interaction among teachers in the middle grades.

The power of these specialists, from an instructional viewpoint, is that they can increase efficiency, promote flexibility, and oversee coordination of instructional efforts. While the administrative specialists in the middle grades could assume traditional roles, alternative roles to aid the instructional program might be:

- Providing leadership in the design, organization and implementation of interdisciplinary programs.
- Serving as a focal point for decision-making activity and school-wide communication concerning instruction.
- Serving as the "official" link to outside resources and interest "publics."

These instructional specialists, and others such as reading specialists, aesthetic specialists, and community resource specialists, support and contribute to the instructional efforts occuring in learning spaces. Each specialist group represents a resource of immense value to teaching teams, and maximizing the contribution of such specialists should be a goal for every middle school curriculum. In diagram form, the role of the middle school specialists is:

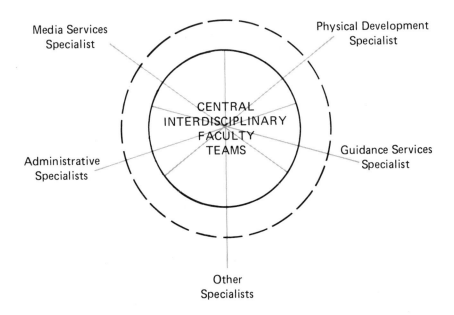

Beyond instruction-related roles to be considered in planning, is the selection and preparation of staff for the middle school. Because the educational programs of the middle school are focused on students rather than subjects, teachers in the middle school must be both committed to students of this age and to an unorthodox style of teaching. Desirable teachers for the middle school would be those who:

see themselves as intermediate level educators
accept and believe in the middle school approach to education
identify with the preadolescent age group
are emphathetic with the problems of preadolescence
understand and respect students of this period
can communicate with preadolescents

In addition to such dispositional attributes, educational programs in the middle school call for teachers who are high-energy individuals who possess such general characteristics as:

44

openness
self-confidence
flexibility
reliability
creativity

While such criteria for the selection of middle school teachers are simple, they are also distinctive. Not all teachers possess these traits. The teacher who is characterized by defensiveness, inflexibility, lack of confidence, basic intellectual sterility, or an inability to relate to students should not attempt to teach in the middle school. Teachers in the middle must be people with a potential to grow and develop along with their students.

In addition to these personal characteristics, teachers in the middle school need to possess basic understandings and skills which will allow them to engage the program. Among major understandings are:

> to understand the philosophic intention of the middle school in relation to other forms of American schooling
> to know the developmental patterns of preadolescents including physical, intellectual, social and emotional dimensions
> to have knowledge of teaching-learning styles which feature two-way communication and interaction
> to understand the uses of knowledge and information bases in the middle school

Among the major teaching skills needed by teachers in the middle school are:

techniques for counseling individual learners
identifying appropriate teaching resources
teaching communication skills such as reading and listening
techniques for using value-clarification in the classroom
being able to work with other teachers across subject lines
working with small groups of learners
planning instructional units and learning centers
enhancing the self-concept of learners
evaluating student behaviors and performance

These characteristics, understandings, and skills begin to suggest the early staff development efforts which must be planned for as the middle school program is initiated.

Finally, there are certain instructional arrangements at the teaching level which facilitate the implementation of the middle school concept. Among those most commonly seen in the middle schools are instructional resource centers, flexible scheduling, cooperative teaching, variable student grouping, learning centers, and the use of student contracts.

An Instructional Resource Center—(IRC)

Somewhere within the middle school there is a need for an area which serves as an extension of learning opportunities found in other spaces. This area, usually called an instructional resource center or instructional materials center (IMC), houses materials and spaces which allow for independent study and in-depth exploration. The IRC also serves as a common site for all activities occuring in the instructional program of the school.

Flexible Scheduling

Many middle schools utilize some form of modular or flexible scheduling to encourage and support discovery learning techniques and an individualization of learning experiences. Each student in the middle school is encouraged to proceed at his or her optimal pace in areas of greatest interest.

Cooperative Teaching

Varied arrangements of teaching staff in instructional settings are used to promote more personal programs for middle school students. The use of "teams" results in synergy—the whole being greater than the sum of the parts. Cooperative teaming building in flexibility and the accessibility of an adult for any pressing students needs.

Variable Student Grouping

Grouping of students according to activity is another arrangement employed by the middle school to achieve its goals. Independent study, studying with a partner, study in small groups, large group activity, and activities for the student body as a whole are used as objectives dictate. While individual study is most concurrent with the philosophy of the middle school in its purest form, peer learning, interest and activity groups, lecture groups and special events groups can also be justified in the pursuit of objectives.

Learning Centers

The search for better methods and techniques to promote learning ultimately focuses on the individual student. In order to release the full capacities of each student, it is necessary to provide an opportunity for unencumbered exploration. The learning center allows for discovery, exploration, and investigation by individual students. Learning centers allow students to perceive themselves as instigators of learning, to discover how to learn, and to take responsibility for learning.

Use of Contracts

Along with IRC and the Learning Center concepts is the increasingly common use of contracts to maximize individual student growth in middle schools and to free the teachers from restrictive traditional roles.

Learning contracts seek to mediate between student needs and teacher expectations. They seek to promote independence in student learning. Contracts attempt to tie the instructional process to the real world of the student by focusing on the process of learning rather than artificial products of learning.

It should be recognized by the reader that middle schools employ a great many curricular and instructional arrangements to carry out the intentions of the program. There is no middle school formula, and the exact combination of arrangements in any given school is dependent on a number of variables. All of the above arrangements, however, can be implemented in any school.

Speaking generally, middle school programs need arrangements which allow for flexibility and physical movement, facilitate interdependence among information bases, promote cooperative instructional planning and teaching, and make possible the individualization of instruction.

Chapter Summary

Planning is a crucial step in the implementation of the middle school design, and one often omitted by districts and schools. It must be recognized that the development of a middle school is a complex and time-consuming task requiring understanding and intensive coordination of effort.

At the district level, a regular sequence of considerations must be faced if long-term success in developing a middle school is to be insured. Districts which confront each suggested consideration will have significantly greater odds for succeeding in implementing the middle school.

At the building level, planners must take steps to coordinate the many arenas of action which will occur simultaneously as the middle school design emerges. A blueprint for planning, such as the developmental staging concept, must be employed to avoid chaos.

In preparing for instruction in the middle school, planners must identify roles and relationships among staff, initiate staff development to facilitate the acquisition of attitudes, understandings, and skills, and must make administrative/logistical arrangements so that new instructional patterns can succeed.

There must be, of course, an extensive coordination of planning at all levels if the middle school program is to resemble the goals of school planners.

SUGGESTED READINGS

Clarke, Sanford. "The Middle School: Specially Trained Teachers Are Vital to Its Success." *The Clearinghouse,* XLV, December, 1971.
Curtis, Thomas E., and Bidwell, Wilma W. "Rationale for Instruction In the Middle School." *Educational Leadership,* XXXVII, 7, March, 1970.
Georgiady, Nicholas P., and Romano, Louis G. "Do You Have a Middle School?" *Educational Leadership,* XXXI, 3, December, 1971.
Lawrence, Gordon. "Measuring Teacher Competencies for the Middle School." *National Elementary Principal,* LI, 3, November, 1971.
Moss, Theodore C. "Characteristics of a Good Middle School." *NASSP Bulletin,* LV, October, 1971.
Pumerantz, P., and Galano, G. *"Establishing Interdisciplinary Teams in Middle Schools."* Parker Publishers, 1972.
Wiles, J.W. "Developmental Staging-In Pursuit of Comprehensive Curriculum Planning." *Middle School Journal.,* VI, 1, Spring, 1975.

NOTES

4
INSTRUCTION IN THE MIDDLE SCHOOL

Instructional patterns in middle school education are unique due to the unique goals of the middle school. Teaching in the middle school presents a startling contrast to other more traditional intermediate programs. Primary differences in the instructional pattern of the middle school come more from the orientation of instructional activity than from the substance of instruction. The middle school represents a new way of educating preadolescents as well as a new form of education.

Middle Schools	Traditional
Recognize and respond to the uniqueness of each learner	Treat learners in a uniform manner
Involve the student in the learning process as an active partner	Give the teacher all responsibility for the learning process
Provide an instructional balance in the emphasis given different realms of development	Possess an overriding concern with intellectual capacity
Integrate informational/knowledge bases in instruction	Emphasize the distinctiveness of subjects/discipliness
Present learning opportunities in many forms through many medias	Present the learning opportunities in standard didactic forms
Emphasize the application of information and skill development	Provide little opportunity to deal with meaning or application
Teach through student interests and needs	Teach according to predetermined organization of information
Define the purpose of instruction in terms of pupil growth	Define the purpose of instruction according to organizational/administrative criteria such as units of credit and graduation requirements
View teachers as guides or facilitators of the learning process	View teachers as subject matter specialists

Utilize support staff as trainers of instructional personnel	View support staff as specialist in narrowly defined roles
Use an exploratory, inquiry, individualized approach to learning and evaluation	Utilize standardized patterns of instruction and evaluation

From the above comparison it can be seen that instruction in the middle school represents a new definition of the teaching/learning process. The new instructional roles are drawn from the philosophy and goals of middle school education and differ from traditional instructional patterns in the following categories:

the purpose of the instructional process itself
beliefs about the capacities of students in learning
roles of teachers and students in the learning process
the way knowledge/information is utilized in formal learning
the means by which learning experiences are organized
the ways in which pupil progress is to be evaluated

The Organization of Learning

In developing learning experiences in the middle school two major concepts of importance are the ideas of continuous progress and guaranteed progress. While the ideal condition for any given student is continuous growth and development in a number of dimensions of growth, the middle school also must ascertain that all students grow and develop. The middle school represents the last general education the student will experience.

Previous educational programs in the intermediate grades have been content to pursue learner growth on a plane, being concerned more with rate of development than with order of development. While rate of development in students is a legitimate concern, to assume a sequence of learning based on uniform materials is to totally ignore learner growth patterns. In the middle school, it is believed that the learner growth pattern is a more logical organizer for curricular sequence than materials.

The middle school seeks to build in continuous instructional progress by focusing on learner developmental growth. The essential thought of a continuous progress plan is that learner development is never static; but always ascending to higher levels of complexity. If the curriculum in the middle school is to keep pace with the learner, and serve all students, the learning design must match learner growth. The learning design must allow for individuality, and must be multi-dimensional to reflect depth of learning as well as rate of learning.

During the past fifteen years, educators have been at work developing "taxonomies" of learning. These taxonomies or heirarchies of learning, have sought to communicate that all modes of learning progress from the simple to the complex. This is true whether the learning is of an intellectual, social-emotional, or physical nature. Learning taxonomies are useful in program planning because they allow us design learning activities for students at a level which corresponds to their development.

An example of developing a continuous progress learning program based on learner growth patterns can be given using two well-known learning taxonomies and sample objectives from the area of academic adequacy.

Below are found two taxonomies of learning. The Cognitive Domain, developed by Bloom and the Affective Domain developed by Krathwohl, are attempts to show a rising complexity of learner responses to stimuli. At the lowest level of response the learner would possess knowledge after having received it. At the highest level of learning, the learner would evaluate the meaning of the knowledge for himself and internalize that knowledge by acting on it. In between these extremes are various stages of dealing with the stimuli either mentally or emotionally.

Bloom's Cognitive Taxonomy	Krathwohl's Affective Taxonomy
Evaluation	Internalizing
Synthesis	Organizing
Analysis	Valuing
Application	Responding
Comprehension	Receiving
Knowledge	

As we look at sample objectives of learning in the area of Academic Adequacy, it is recognized that the objectives are not of equal complexity on these scales.

Cognitive

To develop the ability to carefully criticize and examine information (cognitive 6—Bloom Scale)

To develop disciplined and logical thought processes (cognitive 5—Bloom Scale)

To master computational skills (cognitive 3—Bloom Scale)

To develop a base of information sources (cognitive 1—Bloom Scale)

Affective

To develop an appreciation for learning that will stimulate independent and continuous learning (affective 5—Krathwohl Scale)

To promote and develop one's intellectual curiosity (affective 4) and understand the need for it (affective 2—Krathwohl Scale)

Depth of the Concern

Breadth of the Concern

51

The value of taxonomies and other indices of learning responses to educational planners in the middle school is in their demonstration of how learning activities can be inappropriate. Students have a pattern of readiness for learning, a pattern determined by development in the middle grades, and that pattern is a crucial factor in planning learning experiences. Students can't analyze what they don't comprehend. Students can't internalize what they aren't receiving.

For each student in the middle school there is an optimal sequence of learning and an optimal degree of complexity for any activity. Planners of education in the middle school must view their curriculum in terms of its increasing complexity, and must order the experiences for each student in terms of his development and readiness for that activity. The sequence of the curriculum is focused on the learner, not upon the material.

It is particularly important that planners in the middle school correlate the cognitive and affective dimensions of their programs. Student growth is a function of both dimensions in school, and can be thought of as a diagonal track:

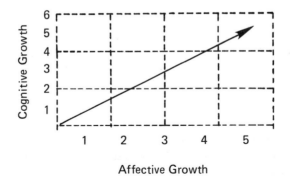

Affective Growth

Continuums of learning in the middle grades can be thought of in terms of information, skills, attitudes, and a host of other concerns of program planners. What is crucial for planning purposes, however, is that the program design recognize the range of learners present and make arrangements for the development of learners within that range.

Because of the immense range of development during the preadolescent period, it is believed that no single standard program can adequately serve all learners. A rule of thumb for the range of intellectual development in school has said to be one year for each year in school. According to this formula, probably conservative, there may be up to an eight year range of achievement among students in the middle grades. A comparable range probably exists in terms of physical, social and emotional development.

Obviously, any responsible program for the middle school must acknowledge and provide for such diversity. One possibility to be considered by planners is the adoption of a minimum-maximum concept of "acceptable progress." The commitment of an educational program with such a perspective is to insure that all students achieve minimal levels of development, while aspiring to assist all learners in achieving their maximum potential development.

The minimum end of the growth continuum recognizes that not all students entering the middle school will be ready to benefit from its programs. This absence of readiness may be a function of readiness, of environment, or poor previous educational experience.

Regardless of the reason, planners in the middle school can expect incoming students who possess identifiable learning problems, who do not have primary learning skills and/or basal knowledge, who have inadequate social maturity, who possess physical defects, and who have had severely deprived aesthetic experiences. These students will be excluded, by an absence of readiness, from full participation in the programs of the middle grades.

The minimum growth expectation for such a student during the middle school would be a curricular experience which would foster a readiness to benefit from later educational experiences. Participation in the school experiences is a minimal goal. While each school would have to develop its own expectations, a sample of a minimal commitment to all learners might be:

- Learning deficiencies (sight, hearing, emotion) will be corrected and learning problems confronted.
- Primary learning skills (reading, computation) will be mastered, basal knowledge learned, and primary attitudes toward learning developed.
- Socially acceptable behavior will be encouraged and rewarded, and each learner will be assisted in forming significant relationships with others.
- Each learner will be given an opportunity to discover his own personal identity, to explore adult roles, and to develop personal interests.
- Each learner will be given an opportunity to experience sensory discovery and to uncover latent talents.

While these goals may seem modest for a student emerging from a program of education in the middle school they are, in fact, ambitious. Our present intermediate programs house thousands of preadolescents who possess none of these minimal capacities.

The discrimination of many school curriculums is not limited to those students who are academically or socially delayed in their development. We also often fail to accomodate those pupils who are, because of superior

53

educational preparation, maturity, or environment, far advanced in their development. There are students entering the middle school who are literate, healthy, socially mature, talented, and self-confident. The curriculum in the middle school must also make provision for these students.

An adequate school program must provide for advanced study opportunities, career exploration, value clarification, talent development, and for the pursuit of individual health-related activity. While each school must assess and develop its own individual commitment to a program of development for learners, sample maximum goals might be:

- To allow for advanced study in academic areas of interest, and for the specialization and development of academic talents.
- To provide opportunities for increasing learner independence and autonomy, and to assist in the exploration of adult roles.
- To assist learners in the development of skills and interest pursuant to better health.
- To assist learners in value clarificaion activities leading to greater self-awareness, career possibilities, and the expansion of interests.
- To allow for the development and advanced study of aesthetic talents and for the exploration of individual leisure-time activities.

The concept of a minimum and maximun thrust in the middle school curriculum is an attempt to develop learning activities which can benefit all learners. Such a design would span remediation, on the one hand, to expansion of potential on the other.

It would be incorrect for the middle school curriculum specialist to think of any one student as being completely on either end of such a continuum. Growth and development patterns in this age group are simply too unpredictable for that. It is probable, rather, that an individual student would present a mixed profile of development for any planning of classroom experience. The individual student may be concerned with minimal achievement in one dimension of development and with maximum achievement in another. A hypothetical profile of student growth might resemble the graph on the next page.

Learning Designs

In addition to providing a multi-dimensional instructional program which will serve all learners in attendence, middle school planners must develop new designs for learning which will tie the school to the needs of the

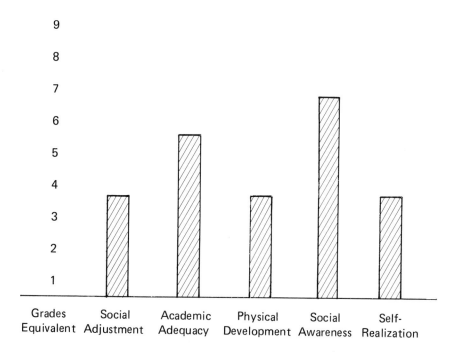

```
9

8

7

6

5

4

3

2

1
```

| Grades Equivalent | Social Adjustment | Academic Adequacy | Physical Development | Social Awareness | Self-Realization |

individual student. Traditional learning designs will not serve the middle school.

In schools throughout the United States, fairly standard learning designs can be found at the classroom level. While many such designs are not the result of conscious planning by teachers, they often are the product of established philosophical positions regarding the purpose of educating.

Three exceptionally well-known designs often found in the middle grades, are knowledge-based designs. That is, they gain their rationale or order from the assumption that education exists to transmit knowledge. While these designs have been given many names, we can refer to them by their design as "building blocks," "branching," and "spiral" curriculums.

The building blocks design takes a clearly defined body of knowledge and orders it into a pyramidlike arrangement. Students are taught foundational material which leads to more complex and specialized knowledge. Deviations from this prescribed course are not allowed because the end-product of the learning design is known in advance. Equally, activities which do not contribute directly to this directed path are not allowed due to the "efficiency" of the model. Such designs represent the most traditional knowledge-based designs.

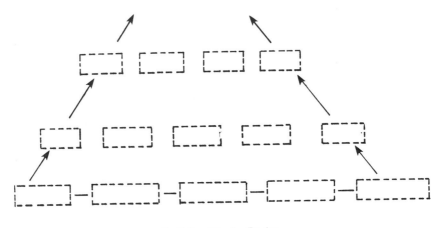

Building Blocks Design

Another very common learning design found in schools is the branching design. Branching is a variation of the building blocks design but incorporates limited choices in terms of what is to be learned. This plan, too, recognizes the value of foundational material that must be mastered by all, but allows choice within prescribed areas beyond that common experience. Like the building blocks design, branching prescribes the eventual outcomes of the learning experience, although the prescription is multiple rather than uniform. In terms of classroom activities, this design allows for some variation but again within tightly defined boundaries of acceptance.

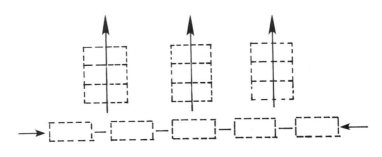

Branching Design

Yet a third common knowledge-based design found in schools is the "spiral" configuration. According to this design, learning in specified areas is continually revisited at higher and higher levels of complexity. While the "tightness" of this design is more difficult to observe, it does in fact control what is taught, and even predetermined the timing of the delivery to the student. Classroom activity is, of course, developed to fit the topics being "uncovered."

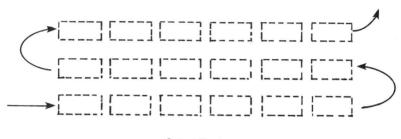

Spiral Design

In visiting a classroom in the middle grades, an observer might see any of the three described designs in operation. In the building blocks design, all students would be experiencing nearly the same program of learning, at the same time, with the same outcome expectations, and with few if any distracting extracurricular learning activities. In the branching classroom, students might be grouped according to academic destination and engaged in different activities within the room. The activities, nonetheless, would be predetermined and directed toward future learning experiences. In the spiral classroom, learning would appear like the building block design, but would use increasingly diverse and sophisticated "methods" to achieve the planned outcome.

All three of these common intermediate learning designs operate from the assumption that education is the act of becoming schooled in specified bodies of knowledge. Because of this basic assumption, these designs are restricted in their ability to gear learning to the needs of the individual student. They cannot individualize the instructional process because they cannot significantly deviate from predetermined learning expectations.

The knowledge-based learning designs are characterezed by set bodies of knowledge to be mastered, uninversal experiences for students, standardized learning enviornments, and tightly defined learning outcome expectations. They do not exist to serve the learner, but rather to serve tradition and the heirarchy of knowledge-based learning.

Throughout this book, there has been an assumption made that the curriculum for the middle school should be designed to serve the learner experiencing the program. Because of this assumption, we have looked at philosophic possibilities, ways of assessing common needs of learners, theories of learning which are individualized, and arrangements that schools can make at the building level to prepare for such a personalized approach to learning. It is the belief of the author that if we are to develop a program of education which is meaningful for students in the middle school we must abandon the knowledge-based designs and refocus our perspective of the learning experience.

The Process Pattern Design

An alternative design to those traditional knowledge-based designs is what will be called the "process-pattern" learning design. The process-pattern design is, as the name implies, a design which seeks to define education as a process, and school as a medium for learning. It is a design which attempts to focus learning on each student and his experience, rather than on a predetermined body of information. It is a design concerned with "how" learning occurs more than "what" knowledge is mastered. As such, the process-pattern design seeks to redefine the purpose of schooling in a philosophical sense, by making education serve the learner as an individual.

The essential concept underlying the process-pattern curriculum is that, in terms of ultimate objectives, the purpose of education is to enable each learner to understand his or herself, to become whatever he or she is capable of as an individual, and to find ways to allow those capacities and talents to serve society as a whole. Schools, as institutions of society, are mediums for that process.

It is believed that the process of becoming educated, by this definition, must be an individual phenomenon. To design a learning environment, relevant to all students, we must have a highly individualized environment, characterized by flexibility and open-ended outcomes. In terms of design, the process-pattern curriculum seeks to set up learning opportunities, to guide the "delivery" or medium of learning, and to emphasize the meaning of the experience.

In schemata form, the process-pattern design is a series of repeating arrangements designed to teach skills and meet needs of individual learners.

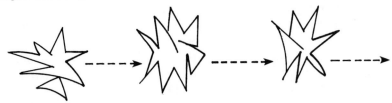

Process-Pattern Design

The process-pattern design can use data about the learners, such as knowledge of the developmental tasks of preadolescents, to focus learning activity. Such student concerns and needs are linked to school-identified learning skills and processes by carefully designed thematic units.

Of course, thematic learning is nothing new. It can be found in many intermediate schools across the country. What is different about the process-pattern curriculum in the middle school, however, is the rationale for the design. The thematic approach is used to bring the learning activity closer to the student so that learning may be personalized and therefore meaningful to the individual.

Thematic learning which is knowledge-based is generally wasteful in terms of time and resources. If the essential knowledge can be clearly identified, then the efficiency of mastery becomes the only variable in the process of learning design. Many "teaching teams" formed in the middle grades along subject matter lines have made this painful discovery. In the middle school process-pattern design, however, there is no such concern with efficiency; only with the effectiveness of the design in promoting individual growth and development in predetemined ways.

The knowledge bases so familiar to all of us do, naturally, have a role to play in the process-pattern curriculum of the middle school. These subject disciplines are time-tested ways of ordering our perspectives of the world about us. The use of these informational frameworks, however, is incidental rather than predetermined. Subjects in the middle school program are perceived as a means rather than an end of learning. As such, they represent simply one more factor to be incorporated into the learning design in the classroom.

It is important to remember that the planning of classroom learning in the middle school should be an extension of previous planning. The middle school philosophy suggests a student-focus learning plan. The arrangements of environmental variables builds in planning flexibility. Finally, a classroom level plan is developed which will enable teachers to work with students in desired ways.

Constructing Process-Pattern Units

The process-pattern unit is similar to units taught in intermediate schools each day except that the primary organizers of the unit are based upon the developmental needs of students and recurrent academic processes rather than predetermined subject matter.

In the process-pattern design, teachers in the classroom construct units of learning activity by manipulating a number of ever-present variables. Included among those variables are those things known about learner needs and interests, skills and processes identified by the school as essential during this period, and manipulative instructional factors which make up the medium of delivery in the classroom.

Eariler in this book the needs and interests of the preadolescent were reviewed under the generic title of "developmental tasks." It was found that all students of this age have similar concerns which are related to "growing up." Among the concerns of late childhood and preadolescence are:

Late Childhood

Mastering communication skills
Building meaningful peer relations
Thinking independently
Acceptance of self
Finding constructive expression outlets
Role projection

Preadolescence

Handling major body changes
Asserting independence from family
Establishing sex role identity
Dealing with peer group relations
Controlling emotions
Construction of a values foundation
Pursuing interest expression
Utilizing new reasoning capacity
Developing acceptable self-concept

These developmental needs and interests of students in the middle grades were then grouped into five broad categories; physical development, academic adequacy, aesthetic expression, social awareness, and self-realization. From these categories, points of intersection by the school were identified. The curriculum program of the middle grades could use the following concerns as organizers for activity:

Physical Development

Promotion of physical and mental health
Physical conditioning and coordination
An understanding of hygiene
An understanding of sexual functioning
An understanding of nutrition

Academic Adequacy

Developing basic literacy
Developing skills for continued learning
An introduction of primary knowledge areas
Development of learning autonomy
Refinement of critical thinking
An exploration of career potential

60

Aesthetic Expression

Stimulation of aesthetic interests
Development of latent artistic talents
Promotion of aesthetic appreciation
Development of leisure activities

Social Awareness

Refinement of social skills
Acceptance of responsibility
Understanding the interdependence of individuals
An exploration of social values
Promotion of human understandings and relations
Developing interpersonal communication skills

Self-Realization

Promoting self-understanding and self-acceptance
Identifying and accentuating personal strengths
Exploration of individual values
Expansion of personal interests

As teachers plan classroom learning activities, these needs and interests of the students serve as "connecters" or "intersectors" into the lives of the learner. They suggest themes or interests which will allow communication with the preadolescent. Specific learning objectives which would aid in the planning of units can be reviewed on pages 19-21.

Another category of variables essential in planning the learning design in the middle school are those skills and processes that teachers feel must be mastered at this level of schooling. While this category of planning variables is totally dependent upon local educational conditions and expectations, the identification of these items can be best achieved by viewing the educational system as a continuum. By the time the student has reached the middle school what skills does he or she possess? What skills are essential, and what skills are desired? Beyond the middle school, what skills and processes must the student possess to fully benefit from learning opportunity? Which of these skills and processes are essential and which are desired? A review of the concepts of "skills heirarchies" and "minimum-maximum expectations" can be found on pages 50-53.

An example of the kinds of skills and processes a teacher might deal with in the middle grades can be extracted from the language arts area. Five major skill areas might be reading, speaking, writing, spelling, and listening. These areas might be made up of the following specific skills:

Reading

Developmental—word analysis, comprehension, structural analysis, phonetic analysis

Functional—locating information, organizing information, interpreting information, evaluating information

Speaking
Informal
Dramatization
Storytelling
Reporting

Writing
Creative writing
Notetaking
Outlining
Letter writing

Spelling
Familiarity
Utilization/application

Listening
Appreciation and enjoyment
Critical and evaluative
Application

As teachers or groups of teachers seek to identify and order those skills and processes which they believe need to be encountered and mastered in the middle grades, it is helpful to initially think of them as isolates rather than as skills needed for particular experiences in the future. Perceiving the skills in isolation will assist the teacher in planning units in the middle grades which are not directed by the specific programs of the high school.

Finally, the teacher engaged in planning units for a process-pattern curriculum must choose among a host of manipulative instructional variables possible in the classroom. Decisions as to which arrangement to employ in a given unit should be made on the basis of the unit's composition. Some of these choices are listed below:

Length of unit
daily
weekly
monthly
quarterly

Unit objective
exposure
familiarity
mastery

analysis
application

Unit Location
classroom
learning resource center
school grounds
immediate community
beyond community

Unit Grouping Patterns	Unit Interaction Pattern
individual study	LRC research/individual explora-tion
paired study	
team study (3-6 students)	question/answer inquiry
small group study (7-20 students)	group question
large group study (over 20 students)	team problem-solving
	creative projection

Unit Medium of Delivery	Unit Student Evaluation
lecture	standardized test/measures
individual reading	teacher made tests/measures
programmed materials	student "sample work" folders
film, videotape, audio cassette	narrative diaries
debate/theatrics	student—teacher contract
outside speaker	progress conferences— project pro-ducts
field trip/visitation	
simulation	criterion-referenced demonstrations

As teachers or teams of teachers ponder these choices and make decisions about the areas of relative emphasis in any given unit, a pattern emerges which is unique in composition but uniform in underlying processes. While the format of units avoids monotony, the essence of the learning experience is regular.

According to the schedule and administrative order of the school district, the teacher-planner should arrive at a number of units to be developed for the coming school year. Somewhere between four and twelve units is probably a workable number for the middle grades.

The task for the the curriculum planner is to weave a design, a multi-dimensional organizational structure, which is made up of a variety of learning activities, learning approaches, learning skills, learning levels, learning objectives, etc., which will facilitate classroom interaction. It is important, given the need to have a balance among the many expectations of the teacher and the needs of the students, to see that greater emphasis is given to certain areas in different units. One unit, for instance, might be focused on the development of learning skills, be dominated by a mastery orientation, and take place primarily in conventional learning areas. Another unit might be more concerned with the development of individual values and perceptions and could occur outside of the traditional learning spaces.

The essential concept, in planning the year as a whole, is to build in diversity and balance in the design. All of those areas deemed important by the planner should be given sufficient attention sometime during the year. The program in the middle grades should be comprehensive.

In developing units, it will be necessary to identify unifying themes which will give an overall cohesion to the varied activities of the unit. Possibilities for such themes are all about us. Thinking of the student and observing interaction patterns among students will assist the teacher in identifying the best themes for a particular classroom. Examples of possibilities might be:

advertising	nostalgia
effects of technology	communication
pollution	the future
transportation	

From such a list, and there are extensive possibilities which reflect the varied interests of the preadolescent, the planner selects a manageable number of themes for the coming school year. In the sample calendar below, five units will be conducted during the year using five general themes:

Sept	Oct	Nov	Dec	Jan	Feb	Mar	Apr	May	Jun

Technology

Advertising

Pollution

Nostalgia

The Future

Once the major themes for the year have been decided upon, the planner begins to construct a learning experience which will achieve both educational objectives and match the needs of the learners. From each major list of variables, the planner selects key ingredients:

Technology Unit

Developing skills for continued learning	
Refinement of critical thinking	**Student Needs**
An exploration of career potential	
Utilization of library resources	
Creative writing	
Notetaking	
Spelling-familiarity	
Analysis of data	**Skills & Processes**
Hypothesizing	
Synthesizing of information	
Charting and graphing	

Eight week unit
Familiarity, analysis, application
Classroom, learning resource center, community
Individual and small group study   Instruction
Individual reading, simulation, field trips
Inquiry technique, problem-solving
Contracts and project products

Following the selection of the key ingredients for the unit, the planner then begins to construct the learning activities which will produce the desired outcomes. For each unit there should be a general plan, and then unifying activities which tie all classroom activity together.

Example: Technology

General Plan

For this unit the students will become a community of people during a period of great technological change (mechanization of America 1800-1840), and will assume an occupation or trade which is representative of the period.

Unifying Activity Week I

All students will investigate life during this period of our national history by attempting to identify an occupation which existed during the era. Attention can be directed to the task of identifying those jobs extending from a previous era, those jobs originating during the era of study due to technological change, and those occupations existing today which date from this period.

Subactivity

Reading of biographies for overview of period
Limited historical research of period
Writing short descriptive essays about occupations of age
Build list of unusual words discovered in research
Identify occupational counterparts in community
Gather comparative statistical data on era under study

Unifying Activity Week II

During the second week, each student will participate in the production of a product or the offering of a service which exemplifies a trade of the period of study. The student may wish to choose an early form of the occupation now held by a parent. Occupational activities may be of three kinds; the realistic production of a commodity, the construction of simulated models, or theoretical treatments of technological questions (ex-

65

ample: why was transportation during this era limited to foot, horse, and sail?).

Subactivity

Discussion about the interrelatedness or work.
Students become "reporters" and interview workers about jobs
Field trips to industry altered by technology
Having parents in as guest speakers on interesting jobs
Conduct "efficiency studies" of workers
Introduce an assembly line in class-make analysis
Charting and graphing of classroom-generated data
Introduce the computer as a tool of man

Unifying Activity Week III

During the third week, students will be asked to draw conclusions about life during this age of change and the effects of technology on their own occupational specialty. The objective of the week will be to develop a set of hypotheses (statements) which each student will individually formulate about work and the effects of technology. These hypotheses will assist the student in clarifying his values and feelings about work. Three major relationships are to be emphasized: the effect of technology on work itself, the ways technological developments can affect community development, and the effects of technological change on the worker.

Subactivity

Set-up assembly line manufacturing, dealing with issues of quality control, over-staffing, strikes within sections, monotony, efficiency, advantages, disadvantages.
Develop a list of "vanishing" jobs in America
Have students develop a "scale of trade" among their jobs based on analysis of the merits of their work.

Unifying Activity Week IV

During this week, students will explore the effects of technological life on a worker. Students will look at such things as specialization in work, degrees of education required, independence versus dependence on-the-job, decision-making autonomy and so forth. The objective of the week will be to get the student thinking about the nature of work, its complexity, its moral implications, and personal preferences of the student toward work.

It may be that during this week the teacher will want to introduce some value-clarification material in order to challenge the students to personalize their observations. For example:

George Sterns is a Master Electrician working in Chicago for local union 1440. He has been assigned by the union to work on a two-year project constructing a high-rise apartment building on Michigan Avenue.

George has always loved electricity. In high school he actually constructed a miniature relay station unassisted. After graduation, George became an apprentice electrician and seventeen months later an electrician journeyman. Last July, George Sterns was awarded the title of Master Electrician after much study. His wife and family are proud of him.

When George reported to the apartment project, the union representative met him at the gate and walked him over to his work station. Located at this site were two small generators run by gasoline engines about the size of those found on a lawn mower. George was puzzled about what he was supposed to do at the site.

Soon, the foreman came along to explain the job to George. His sole responsibility, the foreman explained, was to start the two small engines and insure that they remain running all day. There must be a mistake, George thought. Why pay a man $7.80 per hour to do a job that a child could master?

Later that afternoon, George stopped the union representative to ask him about the assigned task. The representative, surprised at George's attitude, replied that the position was written into the contract months ago. Whatsmore, he added, tomorrow there would be an operating engineer and a pipefitter on the station with George.

Seeing that George was still uneasy, the representative smiled and, nudging George, said, "take it easy Sterns, the union is looking out for you. After all, where else can you get $7.80 for this kind of work?"

Question
What do you think is bothering George Sterns?
How would you have felt if this had happened to you?
Is there anything that George can do?

Subactivity
Have students interview their parents about their jobs.
Try to develop categories of things which separate jobs.
Develop a vocabulary list of words relating to work.

The sample unit could be expanded or contracted in its scope to fit the pattern of the school. It is important to note that in the unit, traditional learning skills such as notetaking, graphing, hypothesizing, spelling and so forth are all taught through the medium of participatory activity. The interest of the student provides the motivational force for more traditional intellectual exercise. Learning ceases to be an artificial product, but rather becomes a process strongly related to the real world.

It can also be noted that in this sample unit on the theme of technology, activities progress through a hierarchy from the simple to the complex. First week activities were concerned with reading, word building, and gathering simple data, while the last week was concerned with the synthesis, analysis, and applications of learning.

As the teacher-planner looks at a number of thematic units during the school year, balance among objectives is important. A unit-objectives grid can assist in assuring such balance:

	Unit I	Unit II	Unit III	Unit IV	Unit V	Unit VI	Unit VII
Student Needs							
1	X		X			X	
2		X		X			X
3	X			X	X		
Skills and Processes							
1		X	X			X	
2	X	X		X	X		
3				X		X	X
Instructional Arrangements							
1	X		X		X		
2		X		X			X
3					X	X	

Teachers constructing such units work through a dozen simple steps that become routine with practice:

1. Themes are identified from student interest inventories.
2. Themes are crossed with existing traditional subject areas.
3. Broad goals for the unit are developed.
4. These goals are assessed in terms of general school objectives.
5. Activities for the unit are brainstormed by students and teachers.
6. Activities fitting school objectives and unit goals are selected.
7. Activities are matched with planning variables such as group size.
8. Overall teaching strategies for activities (inquiry approach) are chosen.

9. Activity "outcomes" are projected by teachers and students.
10. Materials and other resources are gathered for activities in unit.
11. Individual learning responsibilities are assigned for activities.
12. Activities are ordered and scheduled. Unit commences.

In summary, then, the process-pattern design represents a curricular arrangement which allows for flexibility and creativity in teacher planning. Because the design focuses on interaction, on processes rather than products of learning, it can individualize the instructional process. The process-pattern can incorporate the needs, interests, and tasks of preadolescent development. It is, in fact, a complex educational design fitted to the learner. It is philosophically aligned with the goals of education in the middle grades.

Instructional Delivery

The process-pattern unit will not be effective as a learning medium until both teachers and students recognize that they each have new roles and responsibilities in the learning process. Teachers can begin to build this awareness and understanding by doing the following:

- Recognize the crucial role of the affective dimension in learning.
- Begin learning activities in areas familiar to the learner.
- Place instructional emphasis on learning patterns which will have academic application at a later time.
- Actively stimulate intellectual growth through varied experience.
- Be accepting of many kinds of intelligence, especially creative thought.
- Recognize the social quality of school motivation and utilize self and peer interests to school ends.
- Tap ever-present sources of motivation by knowing the needs and interests of individuals.
- Be accepting of many language patterns, recognizing their cultural emphasis.
- Place emphasis on "how" to communicate and allow teachers to be seen as people.
- Realize that groups can aid in the social-emotional growth of students.
- Realize that values are not easily taught but that value formation is promoted by exposing value alternatives.
- Understand the importance of out-of-school activity on classroom learning.
- Acknowledge the power of peer influence and plan accordingly.
- Capitalize on the potential of media as alternative sources of learning.

Chapter Summary

In order to accomplish its goals, instruction in the middle school must be different from previous patterns found in the intermediate school. Middle school instruction seeks to promote multidimensional growth and to assist all learners in their development. Taxonomies of learning and a minimum-maximum orientation can assist in providing depth and breadth in instructional planning.

Instruction in the middle school seeks to set up learning opportunity, guide the delivery of instruction in meaningful ways, and to place emphasis on the meaning of learning experiences. The developmental needs of learners and recurrent academic processes serve as primary organizers for learning. While the learning format in the middle school is varied, the essence of the learning experience is regular.

Learning units are developed by teachers by weaving a interaction design from students needs, academic processes, instructional variables, and knowledge bases. Since the focus of instruction is upon student growth, outcomes for such units are largely open-ended. Such learning units can be called process-pattern units.

Teachers in the middle school must come to perceive the teaching/learning process in new ways if the middle school curriculum is to succeed. They can begin by asking themselves questions about learners and learning in the middle grades.

SUGGESTED READINGS

Alessi, Samual J. and Toepfer, Conrand F. "Guidance in the Middle School: The Teacher-Counselor Team." *Dissemination Services On the Middle Grades,* II, 7, March, 1971.

Bloom, Benjamin S. *Handbook I: Cognitive Domain.* New York: David McKay Company, Inc., 1956.

Classen, R., and Bowman, B. "Toward a Student-Centered Learning Focus: Inventory for Junior High and Middle School Teachers." *Journal of Educational Research,* LXVIII, September, 1974.

Howell, Bruce. "Learning Strategies in the Middle School," Working paper, Tulsa, Oklahoma: Tulsa Public Schools, 1974.

Krathwl, David R. *Handbook II: Affective Domain New York: David McKay Company,,* Inc., 1964.

Riegle, J. Motivating, Organizing, and Conducting Exploratory Activities." *Dissemination Services on the Middle Grades,* VI, March, 1974.

NOTES

5

THE EVALUATION OF
MIDDLE SCHOOL PROGRAMS

Each middle school, because of unique conditions and programs, must develop its own carefully designed evaluation component. To ignore or fail to emphasize evaluation in a middle school will have inevitable consequences for this complex educational design. To survive, middle schools must be able to identify, justify, and document their achievements.

Evaluation as a System

Like the instructional program for students, the evaluation program in a middle school must be comprehensive if it is to acheive its objective; to promote better learning. Like the curriculum, the instructional pattern, and the operation of the school, evaluation should be a product of the objectives of middle school education. Middle school evaluation must be systematic if it is to truly assess the effectiveness of the program.

The primary question in designing systematic evaluation in the middle school is "education for what?" In chapter one the middle school was identified as a school "designed to promote personal growth and development in preadolescent learners." This single purpose defines the parameters of middle school evaluation. Evaluation serves to answer this question: Is preadolescent development being promoted?

As we seek to answer the above question, our evaluative focus shifts to the learning design created to achieve this end, and to the arrangements for learning which have been made. In doing so, middle school evaluation goes beyond the five areas of student growth identified in chapter two to include a much broader range of concerns. Personnel, facilities, learning materials, rules and regulations, and all other program planning considerations become concerns of evaluation. Evaluation in the middle school is defined by the purposes and activities of the middle school program.

One way of viewing evaluation is as a feed-back or corrective mechanism. Here the goals of the school are translated into objectives which in turn create a program design. Student learning, for instance, is structured into activity which has distinct foci. As evidence is gathered and analyzed, discrepancies between desired outcomes and real outcomes are discovered, and adjustments in program are made. Goals are refocused and the feed-back cycle is renewed:

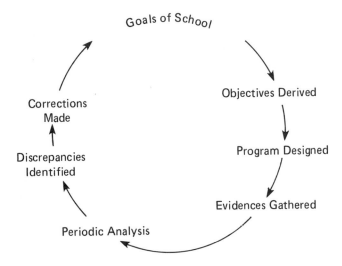

Another way to approach middle school evaluation would be to use evaluation as a means of "validating" program goals and objectives. In this approach, evidences are gathered to justify specific facets of the program and these facets or subsystems collectively comprise the evaluation program. Examples of such subsystems are student performance, teacher effectiveness, program design, resource utilization, facilities usage, policies and regulation, parent and community feedback, and staff development programs.

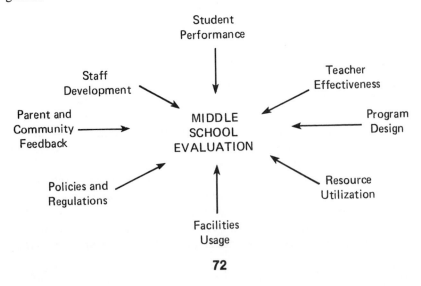

An example of how this approach might work can be drawn from the middle school's concern with teaching academic processes. If, for instance, students were not demonstrating growth in study skills, each area or sub-system could be analyzed for probable cause: i.e., materials for teaching skills are inadequate, teachers need additional training in teaching reading, etc.

By combining these two approaches to evaluation, a school can develop a means of regularly assessing its programs and taking corrective actions where findings are not satisfactory. Some guiding questions in each of the above mentioned areas are provided for study:

Program Design

The overall design of the middle school program can be assessed from both an external and an internal vantage point. Viewed from the perspective of the school district in which the middle school is located, the following questions seem pertinent:

1. Is the middle school concept as described consistent with the overall philosophy of the district and its leaders?
2. Does the middle school articulate (fit) with the preceding elementary programs and the high school programs which follow?
3. Are the resources allocated to the middle school, such as building, staff, monies, materials, commensurate with those given to other levels of schooling?

From an internal perspective, concern for the program design would focus on the structure of the curriculum and the learning opportunities for students. The following questions might guide such an analysis:

4. In what ways does the curriculum actually provide for the intellectual, physical, social and emotional differences of students?
5. What materials and equipment contribute to the development of skills, interests, abilities, and special talents of students?
6. By what means are all of the learning experiences in the school integrated with one another?
7. What provisions are made for student growth and development in health, personality, and character?
8. How are learning activities individualized to meet student needs and interests?
9. What special provisions have been made to insure the mastery of basic learning skills?
10. What adjustments in the organization of the school have been made to promote a "climate" to exploration?

Facilities Usage

Regardless of the age or condition of the facility in which a middle school program is operated, much can be done with a facility to support the advancement of middle school activities. Schools should be built or converted in anticipation of program needs.

While some facility concerns in the middle school are more obvious than others—such as having a building which promotes flexibility and physical movement, which allows for variable grouping of students, and which encourages cooperative planning and teaching—others are subtle. The following questions may assist in illuminating facility usage evaluation in the middle school:

1. Does the allocation of space in the facility, both in location and in volume, reflect program priorities?
2. Is space utilization in the facility flexible enough to allow for individualized instructional activities?
3. Is the instructional resource center (IRC) centrally located and readily accessible to teaching spaces?
4. Are there noisy spaces relatively isolated from needed quiet areas?
5. Is the entire building stimulating in its spatial and color orientation?
6. Are all available spaces, such as stairwell corners and foyers, being used to educate and communicate with students?
7. Is there a sufficient number of special focus areas in the facility—such as darkened projection areas, storage areas for projects, commons areas, and areas for private conversations—to promote program objectives?
8. Is the administrative area accessible to students, teachers, parents, and visitors?
9. Are provisions made for the display of students work, such as tackboards and cork strips in the hallways?

Resource Utilization

The allocation and utilization of resources, both human and material, is a problem area for many middle schools. An all too familiar pattern is to see territorial rights established in buildings, or available resources allocated to favored segents of a program. Middle schools must use all available resources judiciously to promote the program. The following questions suggest some areas worth analyzing:

1. Is there a clear relationship between the allocation of funds and materials in the school, and the curricular objectives of the program?
2. Are staff members assigned to positions in the program according to function and talent rather than credential?

3. Are high priority areas such as skill building given sufficient support in the form of staff and consumable materials?
4. Are resources available, immediately, to support innovative instructional techniques?
5. Is there an established means of assessing future resource needs and planning for the acquisition of such?

Policies and Regulations

Few middle schools regularly view administrative policy and regulation from a program objectives standpoint. Yet, no other single area in a middle school is so important in setting the tone or climate for learning. It is important in evaluation that the following question be asked:

1. What policies and regulations are absolutely essential to the operation of a middle school?
2. What existing rules or policies might contradict the "spirit" of the middle school concept?
3. How might policy-setting and regulation enforcement best be handled to promote the objectives of the school?

Student Performance

Since the terminal objectives of the educative process, in any school at any level, are concerned with student performance or behavior, this area of evaluation is generally given more attention by parents, teachers and administrators. In the middle school, as students are evaluated, we must avoid the folly of redefining the purpose of education while retaining the old yardsticks of measurement.

Middle schools must evaluate student performance in areas that are truly important; areas suggested by the conceptual image of the middle school design. A comprehensive evaluative approach is needed to match the comprehensive educational program. The following question may assist in the development of such an approach:

1. Is student evaluation perceived and conducted as a measure of personal development for each individual student?
2. Is student evaluation both systematic and continuous in nature?
3. Is the student fully involved in the evaluation and measurement of his own growth and development?
4. Is the reported student evaluation social-personal as well as academic?
5. Is the evaluation of student progress related to his own ability and previous performance?
6. Are parents actively involved in the evaluation of their children?
7. Is the gathering of evaluative data comprehensive in nature, such as a combination of periodic testing, student self-report files, teacher-pupil conferences, observations, etc.?

8. Is student progress reporting directional in nature, indicating where improvement is needed?
9. Is student progress reported to parents in a positive manner with emphasis on growth such as in the following scheme?

   C = Commendable Achievement
   S = Satisfactory Achievement
   I   = Improving
   N = Needing more work
   NA = Not Applying

Teacher Effectiveness

Teachers in the middle school are more than simply a resource, they are in fact the medium or delivery system through which the middle school sends its message. Without the full support of the teaching staff, the middle school will falter under the weight of ambition. Full effectiveness from each member of the instructional staff is needed. Evaluation of teacher effectiveness might center around the following questions:

1. Have the talents and abilities of all staff members been fully explored and cataloged?
2. Are members of the instructional and support staffs working where they believe they can be most effective?
3. Are there organizational and administrative constraints on teaching styles in the school?
4. Is there an active mechanism by which teachers can share ideas and activities with other building teachers?
5. Is there an established means for program improvement input by the instructional staff?
6. Does the administration have a mechanism for reviewing teacher growth?

Staff Development

In the middle school evaluation schemata shown earlier, staff development was seen as a corrective device for program improvement. Rather than a regularly scheduled or unfocused treatment which characterizes many in-service programs, staff development efforts in the middle school attack real problems faced by educators. The following questions suggest a possible evaluative focus:

1. Are there monies budgeted for staff development efforts during the school year?
2. Do staff development needs arise from analysis of other areas of evaluation such as student performance and teacher effectiveness?

3. Can staff development efforts be conducted on short notice during the school year?
4. Do teachers regularly have a chance to critique staff development activities and suggest areas of future need?

Parent-Community Feedback

Perhaps the most important dimension in the middle school evaluation system is that which monitors the reactions and interest of parents and the community in which the middle school is located. Without support from both of these groups, at a minimum tacit support, the programs of the middle school cannot fully succeed.

Involvement of the community, like involvement of parents, is a matter of degree as well as frequency. The following question may assist in evaluation of this part of the middle school program:

1. Were members of the community involved in the original study of the middle school concept and the drafting of formative documents?
2. Is there presently in existence a citizens committee at the school whose major function is to communicate to parents and the community about programs at the school?
3. Are members of the community regularly kept informed through school dissemination efforts of changing programs or changes in operation?
4. Can citizens actively participate in school functions at a meaningful level of involvement?

Each of these components of the evaluation "system" are important in terms of program improvement and increased performance by those actively engaged in the operation of the school. All of the components are interrelated and crucial to the other areas.

Student Evaluation

Perhaps the greatest challenge to middle school education is to develop a program of student evaluation equal to the goals of middle school education. If the goals of the middle school are comprehensive, then it is equally important that the evaluation of student performance be broad.

A useful distinction in attempting to develop a conprehensive student evaluation plan is to differentiate between "evaluation" and "validation" of performance. Evaluation generally refers to a judgmental process where decisions are made about the qualitative nature of events. Validation, a more recently developed process used to evaluate many federal programs, is an evidence-gathering and assessment activity. The key difference between evaluation and validation is that in validation, evidences are selected prior to activity so that the determination of progress is a result of objective analysis.

A survey of middle schools by the author has determined a number of student outcomes regularly assessed and measured:

work habits and academic skills
social attitudes and evidences of adjustment
physical and mental health
knowledge acquisition and achievement
creativity—interest expansion—aesthetic appreciations
self-concept and personal philosophy
aspects of critical thinking

These categories, and others, suggest that the middle school evaluate student development in a variety of areas, and that the emphasis of the evaluation program be placed on individual growth rather than comparison to norm-referenced standards. Comparisons to norms, of course, would not make sense in a program seeking individual development.

Finally, it should be noted that student evaluation plays three specific roles in the instructional process. It is a diagnostic device which allows the instructional staff to determine current student growth patterns. It is a descriptive device which allow teachers and parents and students to communicate about the growth and development of the individual student. Finally, evaluation of the student serves to give direction to future learning activity by pinpointing needs. As student evaluation is diagnostic, descriptive, and directional, it serves the learner and the middle school program.

Chapter Summary

While middle schools are student-focused in their orientation, there is .nonetheless a pressing need for specificity in the evaluation of programs. For this complex learning design to survive, it must be able document its achievements.

The middle school can best demonstrate its value as an educational design by focusing on the effects of its highly coordinated program. A systematic assessment of school operations using a validation procedure will provide a better justification for activities than a judgmental process.

In building an evaluation system, each school must select its own criteria for analysis. The philosophy and objectives of middle school education will suggest the parameters of such a system.

Middle schools must pay particular attention to the area of student evaluation since this is the area historically viewed most closely by the public. Within student evaluation, a broad spectrum of evidences are gathered which collectively represent a pattern of individual growth on the part of the student. Such evidences should be used as diagnostic, descriptive, and directional tools in providing feedback about the program being experienced by the student.

SUGGESTED READINGS

Alexander, W. et al. "Guidelines for the Middle School We Need Now." *National Elementary Principal,* LI, 3, November, 1971, 78-89.

Bryan; Clifford; Erickson; and Edsel. "Structural Effects on School Behavior: A Comparison of Middle School and Junior High School Programs." Working Paper, Grand Rapid Public Schools, Grand Rapids, Michigan, June, 1970.

Feyereisen, K.; Fiorino, J.; and Nowak, A. *Supervision and Curriculum Renewal: A System Approach,* Chapters 3 and 7, New York: Appleton-Century Croft, 1970.

Garvelink, Roger H. "The Anatomy of a Good Middle School." *The Clearinghouse,* vol. 48, 2, October, 1973.

Gatewood, T. "What Research Says About the Junior High Versus the Middle School." *North Central Association Quarterly,* Spring, 1971, 264-70.

Wiles, J., and Thomason, J. "Middle School Research 1968-74: A Review of Substantial Studies." *Educational Leadership,* March 1975, 421-23.

Wood, Fred H. "A Comparison of Student Activities in Junior High Schools and Middle Schools." *High School Journal,* LVI, 8, May, 1973, 355-61.

NOTES:

APPENDIX
FACES IN THE CROWD

"Do not imagine that we demand from all men an exact or deep knowledge of all the arts and sciences. This would neither be useful of itself, nor, on account of the shortness of life, can it be attained by any man. For we see that each science is so vast and so complicated that it would occupy the lifetime of even the strongest intellects if they wished to master it . . . however, we must take strong measures that no man in his journey through life may encounter anything so unknown to him that he cannot pass sound judgment upon it and turn it to its proper use without serious error.''—Comenius"

"If we inquire what is the real motive for giving boys a classical education we find it to be simply conformity to public opinion. Men dress their children's minds as they do their bodies, in prevailing fashion.''—Herbert Spencer

"A merely well-informed man is the most useless bore on God's earth.''—-Alfred North Whitehead

"The more a nation has progressed in general education, the more has education passed away from the school to life, making the contents of school meaningless.''—Tolstoy

"For confusion in Education is due ultimately to aimlessness, as much of the conflict is due to an attenpt to follow tradition and yet introduce radically new materials and interest into it—the attempt to superimpose the new on the old.''—John Dewey

"The world of affairs is profoundly disturbed. Momentus social changes seem in process. Civilizations confront epoch-making decisions. Education must face this situation and act appropriately. As we look beneath the surface, what deeper character do we see in the confronting situation? What becomes the task and duty of education? These facts and these questions set the problem for study.''—W.H. Kilpatrick

"When in the year 2000 the historian writes his account of the period through which we are now passing, will he see us in this strange fantastic industrial society repeating formula handed down from an agrarian age when we should be searching with tireless effort for formula suited to the world as it is?"—George Counts

"Even as to industrial achievements, man's free ingenuity strengthened by an education which liberates and broadens the mind is of as great import to technical specialization, for out of these free resources of human intelligence there arises, in managers and workers, the power of adapting themselves to new circumstances and mastering them."—Jacques Maritain

"We must grant that our country has long been afflicted with problems which, though apparently insoluble, must be solved if this nation is to be preserved or to be worth preserving. The problems are not material problems. We may have faith that the vast resources of our land and the technological genius of our people will produce a supply of material goods adequate for the maintenance of that interesting fiction, the American standard of living. No, our problems are moral, intellectual and spiritual. The paradox of starvation in the midst of plenty illustrates the nature of our difficulties. This paradox will not be resolved by technical skill or scientific data. It will be resolved, if it is resolved at all, by wisdom of goodness."—Robert Hutchins

"The only man who is educated is the man who has learned how to learn; the man who has learned how to adapt and change; the man who has realized that no knowledge is secure, that only the process of seeking knowledge gives the basis for security."—Carl Rogers

"The central purpose of an education is constantly one: the universal welfare of man living in culture. And because all others are secondary and instrumental to this purpose, any system of education that so obscures it as to place subjects, drills grades, testing and promotions in the foreground has forgotten its basic role."—Theodore Brameld

"The greatest problems we face as individuals and as societies are no longer questions of food, shelter, and clothing. They are problems of human interaction—how to live with one another and how to find reasons for living in the nonmaterial aspects of human existence."—Arthur Combs

"We need a profound reshaping of education if mankind is to survive in the sort of world that is fast evolving . . . because the forward rush of technology is fast eliminating the cushioning space that once existed between the diverse nations and cultures of the world."—Edwin O. Reischauer

"The weakness of American education . . . is that it educates to the wrong ends . . . it simply never occurs to more than a handful to ask why they are doing what they are doing . . . to think seriously or deeply about the purposes or consequences of education."—Charles Silberman

"Instead of assuming that every subject taught today is taught for a reason, we should begin from the reverse premise: nothing should be included in a required curriculum unless it can be strongly justified in terms of the future. If this means scrapping a substantial part of the formal curriculum, so be it."—Alvin Toffler

"The consumer of precooked knowledge learns to react to knowledge he has acquired rather than to the reality from which a team of experts has abstracted it. If access to reality is always controlled by a therapist and if the learner accepts this control as natural, his entire worldview becomes hygienic and neutral . . . "—Ivan Illich